The
Tape-Recorded
Interview

The Tape-Recorded Interview

A MANUAL FOR
FIELDWORKERS
IN FOLKLORE AND
ORAL HISTORY

Second Edition

Edward D. Ives

The University of Tennessee Press
Knoxville

Second edition © 1995 by The University of Tennessee Press / Knoxville.
All Rights Reserved. Manufactured in the United States of America.
Paper: 1st printing, 1995; 2nd printing, 1997.

First edition, published as *A Manual for Field Workers,* © 1974 by the Northeast
Folklore Society. Revised and enlarged edition © 1980 by The University of
Tennessee Press.

The paper in this book meets the minimum requirements of the
American National Standard for Permanence of Paper for Printed
Library Materials. The binding materials have been chosen for
strength and durability. Printed on recycled paper. ⊗ ✪

Library of Congress Cataloging in Publication Data

Ives, Edward D.
    The tape-recorded interview: a manual for field workers in folklore and
oral history/Edward D. Ives.—2nd ed.
        p.   cm.
    Includes bibliographical references and index
    ISBN 0-87049-878-9 (pbk.: alk. paper)
    1. Folklore—Field work.
    2. Oral History.
    3. Magnetic recorders and recording.
    4. Folklore—Methodology.
    I. Title.
    GR45.5.193   1995
    390'.072—dc20   94-18757

Some things can be done as well as others.
—Sam Patch

Contents

Illustrations

Figures

*Plate*s

# Preface

In June of 1973, *Foxfire*'s Eliot Wigginton asked me to give a lecture on "Collecting and Archiving" to a workshop composed of high school students and their faculty advisers from all over the country (not to mention Haiti and Jamaica) who were interested in beginning Foxfire-type projects of their own. Later, Ann Vick and Brian Beun of IDEAS, cosponsor of the workshop, asked me to amplify my remarks for publication in their newsletter, *Exchange*, which went out to all such projects around the country.

The more I worked on it, the more I saw how much I needed such a guide for my own classes. The result was "A Manual for Field Workers," which I produced in a very simple mimeographed form. In no time at all, I was getting letters from folklorists, oral history types, and prospective foxfirers, inquiring about its availability or asking for a dozen copies, and soon the modest edition was exhausted. However, inquiries continued to come in, and it was therefore decided to issue a slightly augmented form of the manual as volume 15 of *Northeast Folklore* (1974).

I say "slightly augmented," because while the mimeographed form served my own classroom purposes well enough, I now wondered about "broadening" it substantially, in order to make it more generally applicable. Correspondence with several people whose opinions I respected reinforced my own hunch that the manual would probably lose as much as it would gain by becoming much more generalized. Therefore, with the exception of some small changes and additions (such as material on the use of photographs in interviewing), this second edition of the manual remained very little changed from the first, local in focus and specialized to the procedures of the Northeast Archives of Folklore and Oral History. The problems it addressed, though, were much the same problems that fieldworkers anywhere would have to face.

Evidently, many people found our solutions and attempts at solutions helpful because this new version of the manual sold out in less than two years. Meanwhile I had begun to make some needed additions and corrections based on our continued experience here at the Northeast Archives. The most notable addition was an essay on the tape recorder, since I had found that most fieldworkers—especially (but not exclusively) novice fieldworkers—had little or no idea of how one worked or what they could reasonably expect from it. At this point, we at the Northeast Folklore Society were about to consider a new edition, when the University of Tennessee Press decided to publish it as *The Tape-Recorded Interview* (1980).

This time around, however, it was decided not to tie the manual quite so specifically to the Northeast Archives but rather to present material that any archives could fit into its program after adding a few mimeographed pages detailing its own particular procedures. Even so, I continued to use the Northeast Archives as my chief example, just as I used my own field experiences more than those of others, and for the same simple and excellent reason: that is what I know best.

The Tape-Recorded Interview has been very well received, but enough has happened in the past fourteen years to make this second edition desirable. I have made three major changes. First, back in the late 1970s reel-to-reel was still the favored fieldwork format, and since good and reasonably priced reel-to-reel equipment was easily available, that is where I placed my emphasis. Cassette has now almost completely taken over, and I have changed my emphasis accordingly. Second, in chapter 3 ("Processing") I have eliminated the "Complete Catalog" section, transferring much of it to the "Making a Transcript" section. The idea behind making what I called a catalog (an unfortunate word choice to begin with) was to cut down the tedium or expense involved in transcribing, but it simply hasn't worked out that way. People (myself included) got hung up on what to put in, what to leave out, and since material has to be transcribed before it is of much use anyway, I decided one's time would be better spent getting right to it. Third, I have added a brief section on video. There are, of course, other changes. I have updated the bibliography, for instance. But in most major ways *The Tape-Recorded Interview* is pretty much the same book it was.

There are two themes that deserve advance comment. The first is a rather dreary one: my insistence on good bookkeeping techniques at every step—keeping copies of letters, checking and rechecking equipment, maintaining a journal, making complete opening and closing announcements, numbering tapes systematically, keeping track of which picture goes with which interview, transcribing, and the like. None of this is much fun, and all of it may seem peripheral to the real business of interviewing, but it is part of the craft, just as hours of French polishing is part of the guitar-maker's craft. Show me someone who "hasn't time for all that fussing," and you will have shown me someone who really should be doing something else.

My second emphasis is not at all dreary: the common person. People coming to this manual from history, especially from oral history, have often spoken of it as "non-elitist." No question about it, that *is* the Northeast Archives' emphasis, just as it is mine personally. Most of our work has been devoted to documenting the lives of common men and women—woodsmen, river-drivers, fishermen, farmers—and I happen to consider *Let Us Now Praise Famous Men* the sixty-seventh book of the Bible. But that emphasis should in no important way make this book less useful to anyone engaged in "elitist" studies. Elitism/non-elitism is a ridiculous polarity to begin with. Between the two there is no great gulf fixed. No one is common, and "great men" are a dime a dozen, and getting cheaper.

The research method discussed in the following pages involves two separate but interrelated activities. First, it involves going out into the field for extended, tape-recorded interviews with people about some aspect of their experience on which you wish to gather information. Second, it involves processing the tape produced so that its contents will be easily available not only to you but to others who wish to use it in their own research or to check the accuracy of yours. At the very least, that means identifying and documenting the tape systematically, cataloging and indexing it, and placing it in an archives. It also means that at some point the tape will need to be transcribed, either completely or in part. Obviously, oral history is not a short-cut to anything. It is painstaking, time-consuming, and expensive work and involves several steps, all equally important. The actual interview may be the most exciting and dramatic step, but any interview that is not well prepared for or that is not carried out with full regard for the fact that others will be making use of it is going to waste a lot of people's time.

The first decision to be made is whether such a method suits your purposes. It may be that you will do better just taking some notes which you can expand on later, or you may decide that even a notebook is too obtrusive. For example, a student of mine, interested in how her fellow students used proverbs on a day-to-day basis, spent her time simply listening carefully. Later she wrote down what proverbs she had heard, noting where, when, and under what circumstances (by whom, to whom, in connection with what) they were used. The present method would have been useless to her, and any attempt to adapt it would have been an incredible waste of time. Another student wanted to find out how well known a particular legend was in a certain town. He simply went to that town, posing as just what he was (a curious tourist) and started talking to people he met. In a short time he brought together about a dozen versions of the legend by jotting each one down as soon as possible after he heard it. Had he begun by going around with a tape recorder and jamming a mike in people's faces, he probably would have achieved very little except to make a spectacle of himself.

Some people may wish to use the tape recorder simply as an interim note-taker. They will listen to the tape later on, take final notes on what is relevant to their needs, and then either use the tape over again or stick it in the back of a drawer for possible future reference. They will have no intention of placing it in an archive, which means the clarity of the signal or proper documentation are minimal considerations for them. Such users may still find some of the following pages useful.

The present method is not a panacea; it is one way of working amid many. But if you decide that the extended taped interview that has been carefully prepared for, documented, and placed in an archives is the way you want to go, then all of what follows will be relevant, and you can start down the road.

Acknowledgments

Many people have contributed in one way or another to producing this manual, and while a detailed listing of their individual contributions might acknowledge my debts to them more adequately, I hope they will accept the simple listing of their names as at least a token of my gratitude, which is real: Bob Bethke, Gordon Bok, Joan Brooks, Jan Brunvand, John Burrison, George Carey, Mike Chaney, Gould Colman, Jim Denton, Linda Edgerly, Lisa Feldman, Bill Ferris, Lydia Fish, Carl Fleischhauer, Henry Glassie, Joe Hickerson, Louis Iglehart, Flo Ireland, Ernest Kennedy, Waldo Libbey, Fred Liebermann, Dick Lunt, Roger Mitchell, Lyn Montell, Monica Morrison, Gerry Parsons, Sandy Paton, Chuck Perdue, Neil Rosenberg, Dick Tallman, Barre Toelken, Dale Treleven, Ken Whitney, Wig and the gang at Foxfire, and D. K. Wilgus, Cheryl Lavertu and Gerri Moriarty typed the final manuscript and, along with Joan Brooks, helped with the proofreading. Finally, it is entirely appropriate for me at this time to acknowledge a long-standing debt to the late Dick Dorson, the youngest of the grand old men.

For special help on the second edition I would particularly like to thank Barbara Allen, Pamela Dean, Doug DeNatale, David Dunaway, Burt Feintuch, Nick Hawes, David Mould, Lisa Ornstein, Alicia Rouverol, David Taylor, Jeff Titon, and Carlos Vásquez.

ONE

How a Tape Recorder Works

You will not be traveling this road alone. You will have a constant companion, your tape recorder, and you must learn to be at ease with it and to know what it can and cannot be expected to do. To be sure, many people who take pictures don't know anything more about a camera than that you put the film in here and look through there and push this button, but no one who calls himself or herself a *photographer* can afford that kind of ignorance. On that analogy, no one who uses a tape recorder as a tool of his or her trade (as both folklorists and oral historians do) should be allowed to indulge in the dubious luxury of saying, "I don't know much about these gadgets." What follows in this chapter will not make you an expert, but it might keep your constant companion from becoming your nemesis.

We will be talking, here, about tape recorders in general, not any specific machine. You will have to find out how the discussion applies in detail to any machine you may be using, but that will not be a problem. I have tried to avoid technical terms as much as possible, and I am sure I have frequently committed the sin of over-explaining. Yet everything in this chapter grew out of my responses to multitudinous questions, all the way from "How d'ya turn it on?" to "What's that hiss?" Let no one feel insulted by my seeming to belabor the obvious. Each item here was far from obvious to someone.

A tape-recording system has three basic components: the microphone, the recorder itself, and the tape. The microphone transforms sound into a varying electric current, which is then fed into the recorder, where it activates an electromagnet (the "head"). This head then magnetizes a coating of iron oxide on a constantly moving ribbon (the tape), imprinting on it a pattern, the kind of pattern depending on whether the recorder is analog or digital. In analog, a loud sound will make a stronger imprint than a soft one, a high pitch will make a different pattern from a low one, and so on. In digital, the signal is stored on the tape as bits of data—lots of 0s and 1s—in the same way a computer stores information. In either case, when you play the recording back, the process is reversed; the tape runs by the "playback head," which changes the imprinted pattern into electric impulses that drive a speaker, creating sound. Since the magnetic pattern is not destroyed by playing the tape, you can listen to a recording over and over again. When you erase a tape, you "scramble" or "randomize" the magnetic patterns, and you can then use that tape over again. It is as simple as that, if you don't press for too many details.

Cassette versus Reel-to-Reel

Probably the most immediately apparent distinction between different kinds of tape recorders is in the method of supplying the tape. With reel-to-reel machines, you put a full reel on one side, thread the tape past the heads, and attach it to a take-up reel on the other side. With a cassette machine both the supply and the take-up reels are enclosed in a plastic case, which you simply snap into place, automatically putting the tape in position to move past the heads. From the standpoint of how a tape recorder works, there is very little difference between the two; the cassette is simply a specialized kind of reel-to-reel operation. However, since the cassette format has completely taken over the low-to-reasonable price range (unless you consider a couple of thousand dollars reasonable) practically every reader of this manual will be using it. Therefore, what follows will be written in terms of cassette machines, which, by the way, have become sophisticated enough to make them quite the equal of reel-to-reel for fieldwork purposes.

Unfortunately, though, cassette is not as good as open-reel for long-term archival storage, which means that ideally you should make provision to transfer your field-recorded cassettes to open-reel as soon as possible. So long as you have the transfer equipment and either the staff or the time to do the work involved, that is no great problem, but if you don't have either or both, you should at least make cassette safety copies of your originals. It is a second-best bet, but far better than doing nothing. Ultimately, of course, sound archives are going to have to be transferred to something like CD-ROM or find they have been relegated to the Stone Age along with wax cylinders and wire. But that gets us beyond the scope of this manual.

Analog versus DAT

To keep it as simple as possible, analog recording is "old," what we have had all along; it imprints on the tape a continuous magnetic pattern that directly represents the sound being recorded (for example, as a loud sound diminishes, so does the strength of the corresponding magnetic signal on the tape). DAT (Digital Audio Tape), on the other hand, is the "newcomer"; rather than being continuous, it "samples" the incoming sound thousands of times a second and then imprints those samples on the tape as a complex series of pulses or digits (think of the way a movie camera "samples" a motion many times a second, yet is able to reproduce that motion smoothly). Without your knowing any more than this, it should already be clear that the two systems are completely different. Thus people just starting out are going to have to make an important decision early on, and, since it can be a sticky one, let us look at the options.

First and foremost, DAT delivers better quality sound. Its fidelity is nothing short of remarkable, and those distortions that can plague analog users such as wow and flutter, print-through, and tape hiss have been virtually eliminated. Since the tape moves more slowly, you can record up to two hours without changing cassettes. Furthermore, you can copy tapes—and even make copies of copies—with no loss of fidelity or increased tape noise, and you never could do that with analog tapes. Finally, and there need be no question about this, the future belongs to digital—either DAT or some other non-analog form. Change *is* upon us.

DAT has its drawbacks, though. It is, for one thing, considerably more expensive than analog, both in the original purchase price and in the cost of the cassettes; however, as different manufacturers vie for their share of the market, these prices will inevitably come down. But cost—and please keep in mind that I am writing in 1994—is not the biggest problem: digital tape turns out to be a very poor medium for storage. I have heard estimates that the signal can disappear in a couple of years, and even if it is five years that does not compare very well with analog (for instance, I have analog tapes from more than thirty years ago that are still perfectly usable). But that deterioration may be more a nuisance than a real problem. First of all, I have several friends who do their fieldwork using DAT, then dub onto open-reel analog for storage, and they seem very satisfied with this system. Second, since DAT can be dubbed to DAT with no loss of fidelity, all that will be required is re-dubbing every couple of years. Neither solution is perfect, but in all good (and perhaps innocent) faith we can assume that the perfect technology will arrive in due time. Some people I have talked to feel it has already arrived with CD-ROM.

All that I have said so far on this subject may make an analog system seem roughly equivalent to a cuneiform stylus, when nothing could be further from the truth. There are analog cassette recorders available today—small, rugged, utterly dependable—that function splendidly, so well that only an expert could distinguish its product from DAT, and they cost significantly less. The Maine Folklife Center still uses them, and so do I, but change is inevitable. At the moment, though, there are several competing digital systems—one of them using compact-disc technology—coming on the market, and I rather expect that the next ten years will tell us which way the future lies. Meanwhile, unless your consuming interest is recording music—in which case you should consider DAT most seriously—I recommend a good analog recorder for interview work.

How about Stereo?

In principle, stereo is a system using two microphones spaced some distance apart, each mike feeding its signal to a separate tape track. When these tracks are played back together through separate speakers, they give an effect of "roundness," of two ears listening, as it were. Good stereo equipment gives wonderful results, but it is expensive. If one is recording an orchestra, I will say unhesitatingly it gives better results, but in the kind of one-on-one recording most of us do most of the time in folklore and oral history, I don't see that it offers any advantage at all. I will have more to say about stereo later on, but my advice is that you would do better to get the best monophonic machine you can afford, rather than putting money into stereo.[1]

Power Supply

Obviously, in order to run a tape recorder you have to have electricity, and this is supplied by either house current or batteries. Many machines today run on both (that is to say, either), but since the ground rules are a little different for each, we'll take them up separately. House current (110 volt, alternating current, 60 cycles) has the advantage of being essentially constant, but notice that I said *essentially* constant. That is, it doesn't run down the way batteries can, but it does vary by as much as 10 percent—occasionally even more than that. For reasons we need not go into here, these fluctuations are much more common in rural than in urban areas, and while most machines have built-in "capacitors" to compensate for these "surges," they *can* cause noticeable variations in tape speed. All I can say is that in twenty-five years of field recording I have never been bothered by surges, but since other fieldworkers tell me they have been, I mention them here as something you might want to inquire about in the area where you plan to work.

Another disadvantage of house current, again one that seems to occur most frequently in rural areas, is that occasionally your recording will pick up a "hum" from it. I have never had this problem myself, but it has been reported to me by others more than once. If you do use house current and notice a hum you cannot otherwise explain, you may be able to eliminate it by reversing the plug in the wall socket. That failing, try switching to batteries for subsequent recordings.

But perhaps the biggest disadvantage of depending on house current is that it tethers you to available electrical outlets; that is, you have to take their location into account when you decide where you are going to hold the interview. In modern houses that isn't apt to be a problem, but in older ones—especially those built before the days of electricity—you may discover that there is only one base socket in the room where you are going to hold the interview, and that is already overloaded by the television set and two lamps. For this reason, I always make an extension cord part of my standard equipment when I set out to interview someone new. And by the way, the power cord is usually a separate accessory for most small machines, not something permanently attached, and it is very easy to overlook in the rush of preparing for the interview.

It is probably clear by now that I recommend using batteries whenever possible. You don't have to worry about the location of outlets, and you don't have to unplug your interviewee's TV to set up your tape recorder. The greatest advantage is that you can move around freely. I remember one time when a man wanted to show me where an old sawmill had been; I was able to continue the interview as we drove along in the car and as we walked among the remains of the old mill itself. Battery operation is convenient and flexible, no doubt about it, but like all flexible conveniences it has its own set of problems.

The big problem with batteries is that they have a nasty tendency to run down, which is so say they lose power with use, causing the tape to run more slowly than it should (this leads to the "chipmunk" effect when you play the tape back later at proper speed). Many tape recorders automatically adjust for this power loss, but you can count on that adjustment only up to a certain point. I have never known a machine that would not slow down when the batteries became weak. Now all battery-operated machines have visual battery-strength indicators built into them, which is a big help; sometimes, however, batteries will be fine at the beginning of an interview but fade without your knowing it as the interview progresses. Even if you train yourself (as you should) to check the indicator several times during the interview, the discovery that the batteries have faded leaves you with the dilemma of proceeding and making the best of the situation, or putting in a new set of batteries or switching over to house current in the middle of the interview. The chance of battery failure is about ten times that of a "power surge," and for this reason alone I used to recommend the use of house current whenever possible. But I finally discovered that for some three years I had not followed my own advice, with absolutely no resultant battery problems.

The difficulty, of course, is not with the batteries but with the operator. Batteries will serve you well, so long as you know what you can expect them to deliver *and then stay well within the limits of those expectations.* Sometimes the manufacturer of the battery will publish life-expectancy figures (occasionally right on the battery), but almost always the directions for the tape recorder will contain such information. Play it safe: read these suggestions as maximum expectations.

There are two basic principles that should never be forgotten when you are using batteries. First, they are meant for intermittent, occasional use (an hour or two at a time), not for extended power supply. Second, they will recuperate when not in service. It will be best, then, to use them for a short period, then put them aside for a considerably longer period. Of course recuperation is never complete, and the older a set of batteries gets, the less you should expect from it. It might not be a bad idea to pick up an inexpensive battery tester and run a quick check with it before you set out. But, whatever else you do, keep careful track of how many hours you have used a battery, and in this connection I recommend two things: (1) after using a battery, put a small stripe on it with a felt-tip marker for each hour of use, and (2) record the date of purchase on it as well. There is no substitute for the confidence that knowledge can give you.

Batteries vary in type and quality, both affecting how long they last and how well they recuperate. As a rule, the more they cost, the longer they last, but there are several main types you are apt to run into. Carbon-zinc or "flashlight" batteries are sold everywhere, and they are by far the cheapest batteries you can get. In no way can I recommend them. They will serve in a pinch for most work in our line, so long as you only use them for an hour or so each day and then give them overnight to recuperate before using them again. But never count on them for more than about three hours total use. For about half again as much money you can get "heavy-duty" carbon-zinc batteries, and I would trust them for about half again as long. In either case, never leave c-z batteries in your machine for any length of time (like weeks), because they are damnably apt to leak. At the least that makes a mess; at the worst it can cause expensive damage.

Alkaline (manganese dioxide) batteries cost about five times as much as standard flashlight batteries, and they last about four times as long. You can also count on them for longer periods of service, and they require less time to recuperate. In addition, they hold up better when not in use, being less apt to leak (although I would not leave *any* battery in a machine for long, idle stretches).

Nickel-cadmium batteries are sometimes called "rechargeable." They are rather heavy, very expensive, and not usable in all machines. However, if you are in a situation where you have to use your machine for long periods every day, and if you can remember to recharge them properly, one set of these batteries can be used dozens of times over, which in the long run will bring their cost down below even the cost of the cheapest flashlight batteries. By the way, recharging them properly does not mean "topping up" every night. It turns out that rechargeables develop a "memory" and will only deliver power for the amount you topped up, meaning you cannot get at the rest of the load below that. You should only recharge when the batteries are down toward exhaustion. That's a bit of a nuisance, but if you've kept track of how many hours you have used a set, it shouldn't be much of a problem.

To sum up all the information on power supply, I suggest using alkaline batteries, but I also recommend you never go into the field without the power cord, which will allow you to use house current in an emergency. There are many variables, of course (like how long the batteries have been on the dealer's shelf and how tough your particular machine is on batteries), but you can trust a set of alkalines for about sixteen hours, and I wouldn't hesitate to use them for a two-hour session (especially early in their life) or to use them more than once on the same day. Finally, always follow religiously the manufacturer's recommendation on how to recharge batteries or whether to attempt to recharge them at all.

One basic rule will help you get the most out of any batteries: *Never use them for anything but interviews.* Use house current for everything else: cataloging, playback, even fast-forward and rewind if possible (both of which use an astonishing amount of power). With almost all tape recorders, you need not remove the batteries when you change power sources; the house current bypasses them completely, thereby allowing your batteries to recuperate for the next interview.

The Controls

Just about every tape recorder will have the following controls, but their location and arrangement will vary tremendously. You should learn where they are located on your machine—and how to use them. They fall rather neatly into two categories. First, there are the *transport controls,* those that have to do with the mechanical movement of the tape. Second, there are the *electronic controls*, having to do with the quality of the signal. We will take them up in that order.

Transport Controls

Play. Pressing this control starts the tape moving by the heads, and if there is a signal on the tape you will hear it played back. Sometimes this control is marked "play," sometimes "forward" (or even "fwd"), and sometimes simply with an arrow pointing to the right. That is all we need to say about it for now.

Fast forward. This mode is sometimes called "advance," sometimes "ff" or sometimes it is simply marked with a double arrow pointing to the right. Its function is to move the tape ahead in a hurry. On some machines, if you are in "play" mode and press this button you will hear what is on the tape as it races along. This is useful if you are using a cassette you've already started and want to find where you left off. (If your machine has this feature, the button controlling this mode may be marked "Cue," but basically it's just "fast forward" with noise.)

Rewind. Sometimes called "reverse" or just marked with a double arrow pointing to the left, this mode is simply "fast backwards," moving the tape to the left swiftly. On some machines it will be marked "review"; that is still "rewind," but if you engage it while you are in "play" mode it functions as cue-in-reverse, and releasing it returns you automatically to "play." This can be especially handy if you have to use your recorder for transcribing, though I wouldn't recommend such use as a regular thing; if you're going to do your own transcribing, it's best to use a machine built for that purpose).

Pause. This control simply stops the forward motion of the tape without taking the machine out of either "record" or "play" mode, whichever you happen to be in at the time. It is O.K. for brief pauses—seconds, or half a minute maybe—but go to "stop" for extended pauses or you may strain the motor or even stretch the tape. "Pause" is a handy gimmick, but if you engage it, say in response to the interviewee's request to "shut that thing off for a minute," remember to release it when the interview begins again. Forget and you'll wind up with no recording at all!

Stop. No matter what mode you happen to be in, push this button and you will be out of it. Frequently this control operates with a loud click or even a substantial clack, leaving you no doubt that the tape has stopped. No further explanation is necessary, but I do have one suggestion: Except when engaging "cue" or "review" as mentioned above, always switch from one mode to another *by moving through "stop."* That is, if you are recording and want to rewind, always push "stop" first, then "rewind." Manufacturers almost universally suggest that this procedure saves wear and tear on the switches, and it also helps avoid putting excess strain on the tape.

Tape speed. All analog cassette recorders run the tape by the heads at 1-7/8 inches per second, but there are some that have a switch that will cut that speed in half (15/16 i.p.s.), allowing you to get twice as much time on each tape *but with a noticeable loss of fidelity.* Since most transcribing equipment doesn't handle this slower speed, any convenience you gain from the longer playing time will become a nuisance in later processing. *Never* use this slower speed to record music, and I see no reason for using it at all. Leave the switch controlling it on "standard" at all times.

Electronic Controls

We can divide these controls up into those that affect the recording process and those that affect playback only, and we will take them up in that order.

Record. Frequently, though not always, the record button is red or otherwise marked to distinguish it clearly from the others. Get this button pushed and you are making a recording, if you have the mike plugged in (otherwise all you will do is erase whatever happens to be on the tape). I say *"get* it pushed," because it almost always has to be pushed in conjunction with some other button, like "play" or a special safety switch. This "tie in" or "interlock" feature helps to prevent accidental erasures by reminding you of what it is you are about to do. It's a very effective feature, and you'll be glad for it, believe me.

Level. It is this knob that controls the strength of the signal being delivered to the tape, and you adjust it by consulting whatever device your machine has for a level indicator (see below). By the way, for our purposes you can accept the terms "gain," "volume," and "level" as roughly equivalent. Thus, "cutting your gain" or "checking your level" means that you should make some adjustment in volume.

Automatic level control (a.l.c.). Just about every machine has this feature nowadays (in fact, on cheaper machines that is all there is). It means that *you* do not set the record level: it sets itself. If the sound to be recorded gets weaker, a.l.c. ups the gain; if the sound gets louder, it lowers it; in other words, it constantly adjusts the gain to the strength of the incoming sound. Like the point-and-shoot camera, it is altogether ingenious and convenient, but—again like the point-and-shoot camera—it has its limitations and even creates some problems of its own. I used to be fiercely opposed to using a.l.c. under *any* circumstances, but as time went on I found I wasn't always following my own advice, and the wages of my sin weren't that obvious. I still insist that a tape recorder have the option of allowing you to set the level yourself (sometimes called "manual override"), and you should learn to use it. You will usually get better results this way, but, given a quiet ambience and perhaps a clip-on mike, there is no reason for any of us to be afraid of a.l.c. any more. However, you should understand its limitations.

In the first place. a.l.c. should never be used to record music, because it will dampen whatever dynamic relationships (louds and softs) there may be in the performance. Second, you should remember that a.l.c. always adjusts the gain to the loudest sound available to it. If that sound happens to be the interviewee's voice, fine, but a.l.c. is extremely sensitive to background noises (for some reason it seems especially to favor television and radio sound—even from the other room!). Keep in mind that a.l.c. is constantly reaching out for a sound to record, regardless of whether it happens to be a voice or a washing machine, and the ambient noise will swell up to fill any silences that last over a second or so. Then when the interviewee's voice comes in again, it may take a.l.c. a split second to adjust, and that may cause you to lose the first word or so in answer to a question. In addition, I find this swelling up of ambient noise into silences in the interview extremely annoying.

If you have to conduct an interview in a noisy place, the best advice I can offer is to use manual level control, keeping the gain as low as possible and the mike as close to the interviewee's mouth as you can conveniently have it. It is here, by the way, that a lavaliere or clip-on mike is worth its weight in gold (more about this later on). But, to conclude this business on a.l.c., let me say that while I have used it and the results have been satisfactory, I still feel that the best way to use it is not to use it at all.

Voice operated control (v.o.c.). Another dubious blessing—far more dubious than a.l.c. With this feature, the tape only advances when there is sound out there for it to record. If there is silence, it stands still; as soon as there is sound, the tape starts moving again, and it will continue to move until there are a few seconds of silence, at which point it stops to wait for more sound. I see no need for v.o.c. in our line of work. Pauses can be very significant, and with v.o.c. you'll never know how long a pause lasted. Don't use it.

Limiter. No matter how loud the sound you are recording may be, when the limiter is engaged it holds the signal to a certain pre-set level, thus preventing tape overload and distortion. Not all machines have this feature. It is particularly useful for preventing brief "peaks" in recording music—like when a fiddler suddenly bears down with the bow!—but it isn't really of much use in straight interviewing, unless you happen to be interviewing someone who occasionally *shouts* an answer to your question.

High pass/low pass. Some machines have one and not the other, some have both, most have neither. Each is a filter that attenuates certain frequencies, but it doesn't completely cancel them out. I recorded a man in his kitchen one time, and he sat right next to a kerosene stove whose blower kicked in every few minutes, making it difficult sometimes to understand the words to the song he was singing. Had my machine had the "high pass" feature, it would have cut down considerably on that low rumble without affecting the quality of his voice. A "low pass" filter would do the same thing for higher frequencies, say a nasty refrigerator whine. If your machine has either or both of these desirable features, experiment with them at home to find out what they will do for you.

Dolby. Dolby is another noise-reduction device. The versions to be found on the cassette recorders most of us use (Dolby B and C) reduce unwanted high sounds, which will cut down to some extent on tape hiss. One thing to remember is that something that has been recorded with either Dolby B or C must be played back on a machine having these same features in order to reap any benefit. I have never used Dolby myself, and I get various responses from others who have used it. If your recorder has this feature, all I can say is try it and see what you think.

We can now move on to those controls that are inoperative in record mode, having to do only with playback.

Tone. This control adjusts the amount of "bass" or "treble" you will hear in the recorded signal as it is played back. Turning it clockwise (right) usually enhances the treble quality, counterclockwise (left) the bass, while right in the middle is sometimes spoken of as "flat." This control has no effect when you are recording.

Volume. On some machines the same knob controls the volume for both recording and playback. That is, if you are in record mode, it controls the level; if you are in playback mode, it controls the volume of the signal being played back. On most machines, though, there are separate controls for each function, and all I can say at this point is that you should be clear on which is which.

Pitch control. Confusingly, this control is sometimes labeled "tape speed," but its function is entirely different from the switch mentioned above. It is a wheel or dial that allows you to speed the tape up or slow it down by a certain percentage (how much depends on what make machine you're using). *It functions only in playback, never in record* (I have one machine where, thank God, it simply cannot be engaged in record mode, another where you *can* turn the dial but nothing happens). Its only use comes if you happened to record an interview using weak batteries, which would have caused the tape to move more slowly by the head; then you can compensate by slowing the playback speed down, thus avoiding the "chipmunk" effect.

Monitoring. When the monitor is turned on, you can hear what is being recorded played back either through the speaker or through a headset. It is not something you are going to use much, if at all, in our line of work, but you should know about it because of one problem it can cause: feedback. Say you are recording, and you notice that the level is too low, so you turn up the gain. Suddenly the tape recorder starts howling—and that is just the word for it! What is happening is that your tape recorder is acting like a little public address system: The sound picked up by the mike is played through the speaker loudly enough to be picked up again by the mike, whereupon it feeds this signal back into the machine, whereupon it comes out the speaker again, and so forth, until it is amplified into a screech. That is feedback. It can induce panic if you do not know what is causing it, but you can kill it by simply turning the monitor switch to "off."

On three-head machines—ones with physically separate record and playback heads—there is usually a switch that allows you to monitor either "Source" or "Tape," a choice that my students often find puzzling but that is really very useful. In the following explanation, keep in mind that the term "monitoring" is used here not in the sense of listening (you certainly won't be wearing headphones during an interview) but in the sense of watching the level indicator (see below). If you monitor "source," the meter will respond immediately to the incoming signal that is being imprinted on the tape by the record head; if you monitor "tape," the meter will respond to the signal that *has been imprinted* on the tape by the record head, and since the playback head is slightly "downstream" from the record head there will always be a slight delay in the needle's response. My best advice is that after setting your record level in the "source" position, switch over to "tape" for the rest of the interview. In this way, if anything goes wrong—battery failure, faulty tape, whatever—you will know it immediately because the needle will not be moving at all.

Indicators

Position indicator. This device, sometimes called the "index" or "digital counter," can help you locate material on a tape, and it will be useful for transcription work. Always set it to zero at the very beginning of the *tape* (not the beginning of the *interview*). It is of no particular use when you are recording, except that it can tell you where you left off and where to begin again if you remembered to set it at 000 when you started. There are two points of potential confusion, though. First, the indicator does not measure feet, inches, minutes, seconds, or any other standard units. It is simply a *counter*. Second, counter numbers worked out on one brand of machine are not necessarily valid for any other brand. In fact , you can assume they will *not* be. There will even be some variation from machine to machine within one model! But counter numbers established on one machine *can* give you a pretty good *relative* idea of where to find something, even on another machine.

Level indicator. The level indicator is a device that you can look at to find out how well you have adjusted the gain to match the incoming sound signal in order to get the best recording level. On most recorders now it is a meter (commonly called a "VU meter"), a needle that moves up and down a scale on which the left-hand two-thirds is white and the right-hand third red. If you have the gain too low, or if the incoming signal is too weak to record, the needle will remain at rest at the left of the scale. If you have the gain too high, or if the incoming signal is too strong, the needle will spend most of its time over in the red or (in extreme cases) be "pinned" all the way to the right. The trick in getting a good level is to adjust gain to signal so that the needle moves up to the red but not into it, except in occasional moments of sudden loudness someone who has been talking quietly suddenly shouts at the dog). I will have more to say about level later on.

Battery strength indicator. This is almost always displayed as part of the VU meter, but it has its own scale. Usually there is a special button to activate it, and if the needle goes up into the designated "safe" area (and the further up it goes into this area the better), your batteries are probably all right, but it is no substitute for keeping track of battery use, as I have suggested above.

The Tape Transport System

In order for the "heads" either to imprint a signal on the tape or to play back a signal already imprinted, there must be a mechanism to move a supply of tape by the head at a precisely determined and constantly maintained speed. That is the job of the tape transport system, which usually consists of the following visible parts (of course there will be a motor or motors and a series of belts and gears to run the whole works, but the only thing you need to know about them is that they are inside). We will move from left to right.

The supply reel. This is the full reel of tape on the left side of the cassette. When the tape is advancing, the supply reel is not powered, or is powered just enough to prevent it from creating any kind of drag. On "rewind" the motor delivers its main power to this reel.

Capstan and pinch wheel. This is the heart of the whole transport system. The tape passes between the bright metal capstan (which pokes up through a hole in the cassette) and the rubber pinch wheel (or pressure roller), and in either play or record mode the pinch wheel holds the tape tightly against the capstan. It is the powerful little revolving capstan that keeps the tape moving by the heads at exactly the right speed.

Take-up reel. This is the right-hand reel inside the cassette that picks up the tape payed out by the capstan as it comes off the supply reel. It does not pull the tape through the machine; the capstan does that. In fact, during "play" and "record" the take-up reel turns just fast enough to collect the tape passed on by the capstan. On the other hand, during "fast-forward" the full power of the motor is delivered to the take-up reel, and then it *does* pull the tape through.

The Heads

There are three heads: the erase head, the record head, and the playback head. On most machines (but not on the better ones) the record and playback heads are one and the same. In record mode the head prints an image on the tape; in playback mode it responds to the image already printed on the tape. This dual function allows us to talk about three heads, even though we see only two. On the other hand, if your

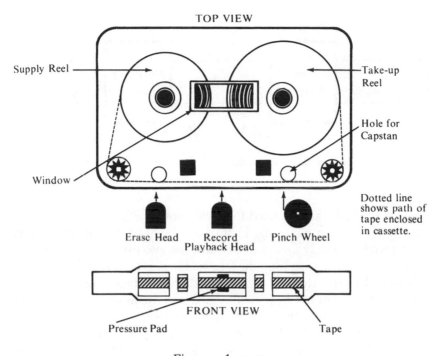

Figure 1. A cassette.

machine has three separate heads, the playback head will be "downstream" from (that is, to the right of) the record head.

The erase head is located on the left, which means that the tape passes over it before it gets to the record/playback head. In playback, the erase head does nothing at all, but in record mode it completely scrambles any pattern that has already been printed on the tape, thereby giving the record head a blank tape to work on. It is always best, though, to begin recording with a clean tape, either one that has been bulk-erased ahead of time or (better yet) a brand new tape, because occasionally the erase head on a machine will not do as clean a job as it should. Still, if you have to use an unerased tape, it should serve well enough.

The record head is the one on the right, and, as was indicated at the onset of this chapter, it is simply a sensitive and responsive electromagnet. It imprints a variety of magnetic patterns on the tape, in response to the varying intensity of the electrical charge, corresponding to the quality and intensity of the sound picked up by the mike. Schematically, the relationship of the heads to the tape in record mode looks like figure 2.

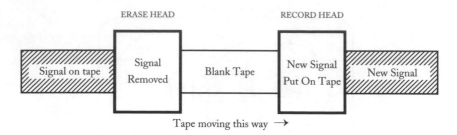

Figure 2. The relationship of the erase and record heads.

That is really all you need to know about the heads, excepting for two things that can go wrong. First of all, the heads are apt to get dirty after a while, not only from ordinary dust but also from a certain amount of the iron oxide coating from the tape rubbing off on them. Since a clear recording requires that the tape be in direct contact with the head, a coating of dirt will not help anything. Clean the heads every once in a while, say after every ten or twenty hours of use. A Q-tip dipped in isopropyl alcohol will do the job nicely, but don't bear down too hard. (Scratch the heads and you will be worse off than before!) You should also clean the tape guides and the capstan in the same way at the same time. And go easy with the alcohol; you don't really need much.

Second, an electromagnet is only a magnet when a charge of electricity is flowing through it. No charge, no magnetism, therefore (in the case of a recording head) no imprint on the tape. But after an electromagnet has been subjected to electrical charges over and over for an extended time, it tends to develop a little residual magnetism, which is to say it becomes a continual magnet, however weak. Now a head with residual magnetism will print something on the tape even when it is not supposed to, and the residual magnetism will also fuzz and distort every signal coming in. Therefore, occasionally—say, every few sessions—get the heads demagnetized, especially if you have been noticing some distortion. You can even learn to do it yourself, with a little gadget you can buy for the purpose.

Half-track, Stereo, and All That

A recording head will lay down a pattern only on that part of the tape with which it comes directly in contact. If the head covers only the upper half, the bottom half will be left unrecorded. Then, when all the tape has run onto the take-up reel, you flip the cassette over, putting

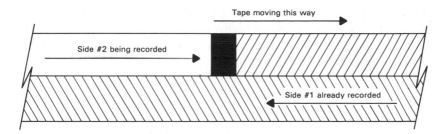

Figure 3. Half-track recording.

the blank lower half in position to move by the head and receive a signal of its own. This is what is called a half-track recording, and it is what we find on almost all monaural machines. (Note: Actually the head is designed to imprint slightly less than half the tape width, enough less to leave a slight blank space down the middle). Schematically a half-track recording looks something like figure 3 (think of the reels as already having been "flipped").

As I pointed out earlier, a stereo machine uses two mikes, each of which lays down a separate track on the tape through its own head. In order to allow for the economy of recording in both directions, most stereo recorders use a four-track system, two in each direction in the following pattern (again, think of the tape as having been "flipped" to begin recording on the second "side"), as seen in figure 4. Thus, tracks one and two are recorded in one direction, three and four in the other.

It is possible to play a stereo cassette on monaural equipment, but the result will be far from stereophonic; it will simply be both channels played at once. Likewise, it is possible to play monaural cassettes on stereo equipment, but all you will be getting is the same thing from each

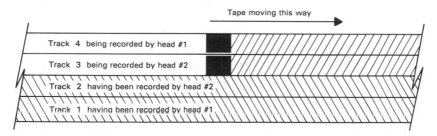

Figure 4. A stereo recording.

of the two speakers. In neither will you be getting the magical separa-
tion and balance that stereo can deliver. Obviously it is best not to mix
the two formats, and I can't think of a good reason why you'd ever be
forced to. But if circumstances conspire, well. . . .

Cassettes

Recording tape is a plastic ribbon made up of four layered components:
(1) the magnetic coating that will carry the actual signal; (2) the plastic
base, the physical "tape" itself; (3) a binder that holds the two together;
and (4) a back coating that reduces slippage and prevents buildup of
magnetic charges where they're not wanted. The last two need no further comment here, but the first two do.

Keep in mind that the perfect base is one that will last forever without getting brittle and will not either break or stretch under normal or
even abnormal conditions. Paper was the first base, but it simply wasn't
tough enough. Then acetate became the standard; it wouldn't stretch
and it was about ten times tougher than paper, but it broke easily, especially as it got older. Then came polyester, which had long shelf life and
proved to be just about unbreakable, but it stretched far too easily, and
many of us stayed with acetate for a long time, preferring a tape that
would break and could be repaired to one that would stretch and
couldn't be. But this stretching problem has been, if not solved, at least
satisfactorily mitigated. Today's polyester bases are just about ideal and
getting better all the time.

Cassettes come in several different sizes (though of course they all
fit into any machine), the easily available ones being designated as C-
30, C-60, C-90, and C-120, depending on how long they will run (a
C-30 will run fifteen minutes on each side, a C-60 thirty minutes, and
so on). C-30 and C-60 are 1/2 mil in thickness while C-90 and C-120
are 1/4 mil, and for that reason alone I recommend C-60. The thinner
the tape, the more print-through (one layer magnetizing adjacent lay-
ers) there is apt to be in storage.

Cassettes also vary in what they use for a magnetic coating. The
three that are generally available are Type I (iron oxide, often spoken of as
"normal"), Type II (chromium dioxide or CRO_2), and Type IV (metal).
Types II and IV are spoken of as "high bias" and require special settings
for their use. If your equipment has those settings available (usually a
labeled button you can push), I would definitely recommend using Type
II; Type IV is much more expensive, and it is not worth the extra money
for interview work. Otherwise, get the best grade of Type I you can

afford ("high output" and "low noise" are helpful designations). And stick to well-known standard brands.

One final thing. Always get cassettes that are held together by screws at the corners. Cassettes don't get tangled very often, but with a screwdriver, a little luck, and a lot of patience you can sometimes straighten things out if one does. On the other hand, if you saved money by buying cheap sealed cassettes, I'll lay ten-to-one you'll never do *that* again!

The Microphone

The "mike" is the device that changes the sound into electrical impulses, and this is not the place to get into a full-scale discussion of how it does that. We will just accept the fact that it does. If a microphone comes with the recorder you have purchased, you can start out by using that one. On the other hand, if you want to improve the quality of your recordings dramatically, especially if you are going to be recording any music, the first thing you should consider is a better mike. But most of the higher-quality recorders do *not* come ready-equipped with a microphone, which means, obviously, that you're going to have to buy one before you can get to work.

Before I get into the subject of better mikes, though, I should say my piece on the built-in mikes—the ones right in the chassis—which I always find a sad second-best to an external mike for two reasons. First, such a mike is doomed to pick up any motor or belt noise generated by the machine itself. Some of them work wonderfully well when the recorder is brand new, but machine noise is inevitable as it ages some. Second, their use almost always forces you to place the recorder at some distance in order best to pick up the interviewee's voice, making it awkward for you to keep an eye on level and make adjustments. The built-in mike is a Great-Idea-That-Should-Be-Forgotten-About. An external mike is in every way better for interviews.

What should you look for, then, in an external mike? There are many different types, but the dynamic ("moving coil") mike is best for our purposes. There are two important elements to consider: impedance and directional characteristics. Impedance is measured in ohms (Ω), and your recorder's specifications should tell you whether it requires a low (measured in the hundreds) or high (measured in the thousands) impedance mike. The match does not have to be perfect; in fact it can be very rough, but if you match a low-impedance mike with a high-impedance input you may find you have to keep your gain unusually high. Since most of the better dynamics are low-impedance, and since that conformation has the added advantage of picking up less hum and other stray noises, a low-impedance mike in the $75 to $150 range is your best bet. If your recorder accepts high-impedance input only, you can get a small "line-matching transformer" for a few dollars that will take care of that problem nicely.

As for directional characteristics, most of the mikes we deal with are of two basic kinds: omnidirectional or cardioid. The omnidirectional mike, as its name implies, is designed to pick up sounds from all directions equally, which means that if you put such a mike halfway between you and your interviewee, it would record your voices at about the same level (assuming your voices are equally strong). Other mikes are made to favor sounds from directly in front of them; their sensitivity drops off as the sound source moves to the sides, and they are least sensitive to sounds from directly behind them. Plot this range on the floor and it comes out in a kind of heart shape, which is why it is called cardioid, with the apex in front, the "dent" directly behind the mike. Both omnidirectional and cardioid mikes have their advantages and disadvantages in interview situations, but it is at least good to know which kind you have. The specifications that accompany your mike will give you this information, but if you have a mike whose pattern you do not know, you can establish it for yourself when you play "the game" described below.

Just where should you place the mike relative to the person you are interviewing? That is something that will vary from mike to mike and machine to machine, not to mention interviewee to interviewee. You should make sure that your voice comes through clearly too, although it need not be at the same level as the interviewee's. Keep this basic principle in mind: the clarity of your recording (and minimizing of extraneous noise) is almost entirely a function of how close you can get the mike to the interviewee's mouth and how low you can keep the gain while still getting a good signal. The further you have the mike from the interviewee and the higher you have to bring up the gain, the more "hollow" the voice will be and the more background noise you will get. But if you hold the mike right up to his or her face, or if you flip it back and forth the way you see television newsmen do, you will create a situation in which neither of you can relax much. You will have to compromise. Perhaps you can set the mike on the little table next to the chair, or even over the back of the chair (I have done that once or twice). Try some of these placements at home and see how they work. But remember the basic principle: Get the mike as close to the interviewee as you can without making it so obtrusive as to be a nuisance.

Recently I have taken to using a small clip-on mike (small meaning about the size of a pencil eraser), and I've been very pleased with the results. It gets the mike about as close to the sound source as you'd ever want to get, it's extremely inconspicuous, and—at least the one I'm using—it's very affordable. A couple of friends tell me they use two of them—one on the interviewee and the other on themselves—with a stereo machine, putting interviewer and interviewee on separate tracks. I haven't tried this rig yet, but I can well believe it is as good as my friends claim, and it is certainly worth mentioning here. Two caveats: first, the clip-on requires a small button-type battery, which you have to remember to turn off when you're not using it, making it just one more thing to keep track of; second, if the person you're interviewing suddenly decides to head upstairs, you're going to have to do a quick rescue job to save your equipment! I should mention, too, that at first I was hesitant to reach into the interviewee's "space" to clip the mike on, but that has turned out to be a non-problem. Besides, worst coming to worst, you can always ask him or her to take care of that for you.

This is probably as good a place as any to stress how very sensitive to extraneous noises a microphone can be. Let me give an example: You are interviewing an elderly man, and his wife says, "Well, I'll just leave you two alone," whereupon she goes into the kitchen and washes the dishes. You hear nothing at all during the interview itself, but later on when you play it back, the crash-bang of the crockery fair to drowns out the interview. Try as best you can to hold the interview in a place where there won't be a lot of background noise. If you think such noise will present a problem, try going ahead with the interview; then say, "Hold it a minute, I just want to see if this machine is working all right," and listen to a little of what you have recorded. If you have a problem, see what can be done about it without upsetting the entire household. But frankly, just being mindful of the possibility of problems of this type will eliminate about two-thirds of them.

"The Game"

In order to learn what your mike can or cannot do—in fact it is a good way to learn the strengths and weaknesses of your recording equipment in general—I recommend the following game. Set the machine up in such a way that you can see the VU meter from some distance away. Put a tape in, set the machine in record mode, and talk, all the time telling yourself what it is you are doing and how the machine is responding at the moment. Something like this (I am assuming you have manual level control, but the game is useful for finding out what automatic level control can do, too):

> Now I've turned the thing on, and I'm talking in my normal voice directly in front of the mike and about two feet from it. The gain is set at 6 and the needle on the VU meter is moving up to but not into the red area. Now I'm moving back to about four feet from the mike and I haven't changed anything else, and the needle is only moving up about a quarter of the way, except when I SHOUT, when it jumps up almost to the red. O.K., now I'm moving over to the right to about forty-five degrees, still about four feet away, and the needle is hardly moving at all, just a little. Now I'm moving in to turn the machine some so I can see the meter from over here—I haven't moved the mike or changed anything else—and O.K. now I'm back out again at four feet, and the needle isn't moving at all now. Now I'm directly behind the mike, and the needle still isn't moving, even when I SHOUT—well, it did move just a little then, but. . . .

Keep this game up, trying different settings and distances, letting your voice be loud and soft, always telling yourself three things: where you are in relation to the mike, what the needle on the VU meter is doing, and what level you have set the gain at. (*Note:* On some machines the gain control is not calibrated, in which case you can use the analogy of a clock face: "I've set it at three o'clock," etc.) Try as many different combinations of control settings as are available to you. If your machine has a built-in mike, try that, and then right after it try the external mike. Try it with Dolby in or out, with high- and low-pass, with and without the limiter. Try it with an electric fan, a vacuum cleaner, a television set in the background. If you have a cardioid mike, what happens when you aim it straight up? Don't hurry the game. Take plenty of time and try everything.

One of the most important things you can learn from this game is how low a level you can record at and still get a decent signal. Start with the gain at zero and move up all the way to the top by steps, giving yourself enough tape to listen to at each step. When you play this section back, you may find that you get a perfectly good signal at ten o'clock, even tough the needle was only moving a little. Since meters vary in sensitivity and get out of adjustment easily, you may find that you get a better recording at low level than when the needle is moving (as it ideally should for the best signal) just up to the red. You will certainly discover what a fuzzy signal you get when you over-record, when the needle stays in the red most of the time.

That brings me to a final note on recording level: it is by far the lesser of two evils to under-record a bit than to over-record. With a weak signal you can always turn the volume up on playback to compensate; you will get more tape noise, of course, but even that is better than the fuzzed-up signal you will get by over-recording—and there is absolutely nothing you can do to correct *that* distortion. Of course, the dilemma is a false one, because with a little care you can record at the proper level almost every time.

Immediate Action: When "It Won't Go"

It is bound to happen sometime, and you can almost count on it occurring just as you are ready to begin your interview: you turn the machine on and nothing happens. Your batteries are in good shape—everything was working fine when you left home this morning. You know your batteries are reasonably fresh, and you know you have not accidentally left the recorder running since the last time you checked it. Now what?

It may be that something in the works *has* "blown" or "burned out," which will mean you are really out of business until you can get it fixed, but the odds are a good ten-to-one against it. Run through the following "immediate action" steps before you can conclude that doomsday has come:

1. If there is an on/off switch on the side of the mike (sometimes called a "servo-" or "remote-control"), check to make sure it is in the "on" position.

2. Check to see if you have accidentally left the "pause" lever engaged. In my experience, this and the preceding (no. 1) will take care of well over half the "won't go" problems.

3. Check the cassette to see if the little tabs that prevent accidental erasure have been broken out. If they have, either get a new cassette or cover the holes with a piece of tape.

4. If you are using house current, check the plug on the recorder end. Wiggle it a little, and give it a good push to assure yourself that it is fully seated. Then do the same thing on the wall outlet end. Try flipping the plug over. If you are satisfied that the problem is not poor contact (and that the cord is not broken), it is just possible that the outlet is at fault. Try plugging a lamp into it (I mention this because there are two outlets in my summer study, neither of which is connected to anything!).

5. If you are using batteries, open the battery compartment and check to see that the batteries are installed properly. Are any of them in backwards? If not, then simply roll the batteries with your hand without re-

moving them; sometimes just a tiny bit of corrosion will form and keep one battery from making complete contact with the next one, and rolling them will be enough to make that contact again. If that fails, simply take the batteries out and put them back in again in a different order. It sounds ridiculous, but it works. Failing that, forget the batteries and plug in to house current.

Some people recommend having a spare set of batteries around—a great idea, but in the thirty years I have been using battery-powered machines I have never (a) remembered to bring them or (b) been inconvenienced by not having them. Others recommend bringing along a back-up tape recorder—another great idea, if you can afford it! Of course, these auxiliary or back-up systems become more necessary the further afield you go and the longer you plan to be away from home. But that is a matter of planning an expedition, not immediate action. For the average day-tripping involved in most of the work readers of this manual will be doing, the five steps I have suggested will make the difference between "no-go" and "go" 90 percent of the time.

If you have simply *read* this far, you already know more about a tape recorder than half the people out using them who say they are "collecting folklore" or "doing oral history." And now if you read carefully the directions that come with your particular machine, and if you will conscientiously play my suggested "game," you will be better prepared to get to work than 75 percent of them—and at least as well prepared as 90 percent of them. That should (in the original and etymological sense of a good old word) *encourage* you some.

TWO

Interviewing

Finding People to Interview

"How do you find these wonderful people?" That is a question I have often been asked, and it implies that "interviewees" are a special kind of animal and that finding them is something like catching night-crawlers: "You gotta be quick!" I often answer that question by saying that everybody is a potential interviewee for something, which is usually accepted as a polite evasion on my part. But my answer is an honest one, and the first thing that you have to do in this line of work is to stop looking for that wonderfully gnarled old woman sitting in front of her foxfire in a just-right squeaking rocking chair and accept the possibility that your neighbor's teen-age son home on vacation from Groton may be a perfect interviewee for what you are interested in. The important thing is to have a very clear idea what it is you want to find out. Once you know that, you will probably have very little trouble finding good people to talk to.

You can begin by "asking around." If, for instance, you have become interested in "Old Dalton," whose stories you can remember your father quoting with great amusement, your father should be the first person you turn to as a possible interviewee: "Remember those stories you used to tell me about Old Dalton? Well, I'm. . . ." Chances are he will balk a bit—"Oh good Lord! You don't want *them*. Why they're nothing but a lot of lies anyhow!"—but if you persist and make it clear what you are doing, all will be well. One person will lead to another, usually: "Your Uncle Floyd knows a lot more of those stories than I do. Why don't you go see him?" Fine, go see Uncle Floyd, but only after you have made it clear to your father that you want the stories the way *he* remembers them too. Accept such references as new prospects, but never let this "handing on" become a "putting off." You will not only not find the pot of gold, you will probably lose the rainbow as well.[2]

I have warned against searching for the perfect or ultimate interviewee, but that is not to say there won't be special people you should see. You may know someone who is an exceptional storyteller or a singer with a considerable local reputation. You should of course see these people, but the point is that you should not spend all your valuable time looking for such perfection when the stuff of folklore and local history is alive all around you.

One of the best methods I know is to publish a letter in whatever newspaper it is that people in that area read, or write an article and ask the editor if he will use it in a coming edition. In that letter be as specific as you can about what it is you are looking for, while at the same time being careful not to "lead" by giving the very information you hope to get. If you are looking for information on that "notorious liar," I would advise against calling him "probably the most famous story-teller in these parts," because it is possible there are others far better known that by some cultural coincidence you simply have not heard of. I also advise against saying you are "writing a book." That phrase conjures up all sorts of sugar-plum visions in people's heads, and it may discourage some from responding because they are convinced that they do not know enough to be able to help you. Let it be known that you have heard of this man and the stories he used to tell, that you will be visiting the area soon, and that you would like to hear ("at the address given below") from anyone who can tell you anything at all about the man or his stories.

I have had great success with this simple ploy. In writing about the lumberwoods songmakers Larry Gorman and Joe Scott, since their "community" was actually all of Maine and the Maritime Provinces of Canada, I published such letters in practically every daily and weekly newspaper in the area, and I received dozens of responses. In writing about Lawrence Doyle, since his tradition was pretty well limited to Prince Edward Island, I only published a letter in the Charlottetown (P.E.I.) *Guardian,* and here again I got excellent results, I even heard from many people off the Island who told me that someone "back home" had clipped my letter and sent it on to them.[3]

Some of my best interviewees have come to me *via* the newspaper letter, but not everyone who writes in is going to be a good interviewee, of course. Unfortunately, there are a lot of inveterate letter-writers in the world, people who evidently write simply to write. But don't take chances by sorting people out before meeting them; the only thing you can do is see them all. Some excellent sources sound impossible in their letters. It also happens that a lot of people will write you not because *they* know something but because they *know* someone who does (though this

may not be clear in their letters). In other words, they are good secondary sources. And that leads me to mention another great advantage of
the newspaper letter: it alerts many people who would not write themselves but who nevertheless will see the letter. Frequently, on the recommendation of secondary sources, I have gone to see people and had
them say, "Oh yes, you're the fella that's interested in Lawrence Doyle.
How are you making out?" That was said with genuine interest, and
they often added that they didn't write me because they didn't feel that they
had enough information or because everyone knew what they knew.

I have yet to find a situation where my letter to the newspaper has
worked against me in any way. First of all, it has found me many good
interviewees, both directly and indirectly. Second, it has allowed me to
go into a strange area with some sort of identity. I have specific people
to go see, and when I see them I have something specific to talk about.
I may be a stranger, but there is nothing mysterious about me at all.

Two further bits of advice on newspaper letters will be helpful. Ask
the paper to send you a dated clipping of your letter (include a stamped
self-addressed envelope with your request). And promptly answer every
letter that comes to you, keeping a copy of your reply. In other words,
keep good records. I wouldn't mention this, except that I know from
experience it is too easy *not* to do; and if you don't, you can be sure you
will be sorry for it at some point.

And a final warning: people will sometimes direct you to the local
historian, saying that he or she "has a lot of that old stuff." Unfortunately, many local historians have little understanding of and even less
interest in the kind of material you will be looking for. Many of them
are still caught up in "great man/significant event" history and will not
consider a local farmer who used to make up songs important enough
for their attention. Nor will they be much help when it comes to folklore, much of which, as far as they are concerned, is simply "not true."
But there are splendid exceptions, and such exceptions can be a tremen-
dous help in suggesting people to see, things to check out, and the like.
Besides, many local historians have devoted years to gathering material,
often with little thanks, and it would be both rude and pointless not to
consult with them.

The Initial Contact

Assuming, then, that you have become well-acquainted with your tape
recorder, that you know what it is you want to find out, and that you
have the names of people you want to see, your first job is to break the

ice and make an appointment with your prospective interviewee. I have
found it a good idea to write a letter first (see my sample letter in the Appendix): not only is it polite, it identifies you very well and gives the person
something to think about. If your work is being sponsored by some orga-
nization (say a college or some local group) whose letterhead stationery you
can use, it helps some by giving you a sort of instant respectability.

Once you have sent the letter, wait a few days and then follow up
with either a phone call or a visit (or both) to make arrangements for
the first interview. Don't call too soon; give the letter enough time to
get there and the prospect enough time to consider it. And don't wait
too long; in either case you lose the real value of writing the letter. As a
rule of thumb, let the letter arrive, then wait one or two days, but never
wait more than a week.

Of course, a letter may be much more than is required. You may
already know the prospect, or he or she may contact you first (say in response to your newspaper letter), or a third party (say a son or a daugh-
ter) may encourage you just to call or drop in ("Mother's always home
and I know she'd be delighted to talk to you"). Such arrangements are
fine, and they probably will work out all right, but it never hurts to be a
little circumspect in the face of such encouragement. If it sounds like a
good lead, and if you are reasonably certain that the person making the reference knows what you are doing, you might ask that person to call on your
behalf. Generally, I prefer to keep things in my own hands, though, by calling myself. And if time and circumstances permit, I write a letter.

Some people tell me they hesitate to write a formal letter because
they "don't want to get the poor soul all worked up." I suppose it could
work out that way, but I have never known it to. Others have said that
if they write—or even call—the prospect has more of a chance to say
no, while if they just drop in the battle is half won already. There may
be special circumstances where the surprise attack is justified, but it *is*
pushy, and I avoid it whenever I can (which is almost all the time!). Besides, you would normally write an opening letter to a retired general or
an actor you wished to talk to; why not offer the same courtesy to a la-
boring man or a farm wife?

Generally, then, a letter followed by a phone call is ideal. A letter
alone is all right (and of course if there is no phone it is all you *can* do).
A phone call alone may be all that is required, but think carefully about
why you are not going to bother with a letter. Finally, try not to arrive
on someone's doorstep unannounced in any way; it may be necessary,
but it usually is not.

There are two questions that students often ask at about this point.

The first, and by far the more common, frequently comes out something like this: "Do you think it's going to make a difference that I'm a girl when I go talk to Mr. Bilodeau about lumbering?" My answer is usually, "Of course it's going to make a difference, but I can't tell you what kind of difference." I have seen it happen that a man who was reluctant to talk to a woman at first came very quickly to enjoy the whole thing thoroughly once he discovered that she knew what she (and, of course, he) was talking about. Sometimes a woman will open up to a male interviewer after she had been very careful and even shut-mouthed with a female. Just about every time I have predicted how the man/woman of it would work out in some particular case, I have been wrong, which means that I have stopped predicting. All I can suggest is that you be sensitive to this problem, but no one should ever be scared out of attempting an interview because of it. It is much more important that the interviewee have confidence that the interviewer knows what he or she is talking about, and a recent incident speaks to that point. Two girls had gone at different times to interview a man in connection with our work on Argyle Boom.[4] At a later time I went to see him myself. "I'm glad you're here," he said. "You know, it's kind of hard to explain these things to a girl." What he told me was just about the same as what he had told them, which they had understood thoroughly. In other words, the difference in interviewers had no effect on the success of the interview, even though the interviewee thought it did.

The second question is only a bit different from the first: "Wouldn't it be better if Edgar went to interview Mr. Bresnahan? I mean, that's his uncle, after all." The answer is, "Maybe, but not necessarily." The rationale behind the question is that Edgar won't have to go through the ice-breaking and will know better what to ask. The rationale behind the answer is that there is much Edgar won't ask, because he already knows all about it, and Mr. Bresnahan won't explain some things for the same reason. There is something called "stranger value," which means that none of these assumptions exist between people who don't know each other, and sometimes people will say things to strangers that they would feel awkward or silly saying to members of the family. It's kind of a paradox, but people frequently find that being interviewed by a close friend or relative is an odd and not entirely pleasant experience, while they will feel more at ease with a stranger under the same circumstances. The paradox is less obvious if you are asking for specific items like stories or songs than if you are after more general cultural information, but it is still there. I would far prefer to interview a stranger, myself, but there are plenty of examples of successful interviewing of close relatives and friends.

When you make your appointment for the preliminary interview, be sure the time and place are clear to both of you. Do you need directions to reach the house? What time is convenient? May you bring a friend (if that is part of your plans)? If you can, send a quick note confirming the time, place, and circumstances you have both agreed to. If there seemed to be any vagueness about the appointment ("Next Friday afternoon? Yeah, I'll probably be here all right"), you might want to call the day before and check for sure. If you still get a "probably," there is little to be done, because you can hardly insist. But that is simply a way of speaking some people have, and I can assure you the person "probably" *will* be there. Risk it. And even if you think you are sure of your directions, allow plenty of time for getting lost the first time out.

What do you do about a "no show"—you're there at the appointed time but the interviewee is not? Since you are the one looking for his or her help, there isn't much you *can* do except go home and try again. Always make the most charitable assumption you can, and work from there. There are so many possibilities: forgetfulness, for instance, or sudden busy-ness, or it may be that appointments do not carry the same weight in that culture or subculture as they do in yours. Whatever you do, don't cross that person off your list in a fit of pique. Be patient.

The Preliminary Interview

You have made your initial contact by phone, letter, or both, and now here you are on the doorstep, about to meet the interviewee for the first time. I have always found this the most anxious moment of the whole game: the time when I actually come face-to-face with my prospect. I have practiced all kinds of self-deceptions so that I could put it off for an hour or a day ("I'm going into town for a cup of coffee first,". . . "Morning's a bad time.". . .), a point I would not bother to mention except that the novice may take some comfort in realizing that the so-called expert gets the same butterflies in his stomach for the same reason—and always will. But if you have made your initial contact by letter, phone, or both, you may also take comfort in knowing that the worst is already over, and you are not arriving a perfect stranger.

The preliminary interview is several things at once. It is, first of all, a time for you and the interviewee to get acquainted, but it is also a time when you can answer questions and explain more fully what it is you are doing and decide whether or not this particular prospective interviewee is in fact a good interviewee. We will take up the last of these considerations in more detail.

There are two basic questions you can use as guides. First, *does this person actually have the information you are looking for?* If, for example, the person has been recommended to you as someone who has a lot of old songs, is that information correct? I once went to see a woman on such a lead, only to have her show me a pile of old sheet music on top of the piano while admitting that she herself did not sing. On another occasion I went to see a man who told me he had known Lawrence Doyle, only to discover that he had been born the year Doyle died. I should add that in this case the man turned out to know a lot of Doyle's songs and had heard a lot about him from his parents and older neighbors, which made him a very valuable interviewee anyhow. It simply meant that his eyewitness accounts were something less than that. (By the way, I never "confronted" him with what I knew, which would have been to call him a liar. I simply kept what I knew in mind.)

Assuming that the prospect has the information you seek, your second question can follow: *Is this person willing and able to share that information with you?* You may find people who, for any one of a number of reasons or for no apparent reason at all, are simply not interested in talking with you. You may also find people who, no matter how hard you try to persuade them or what assurances you offer them, clearly want to avoid talking with you. It may be that the person is too busy, although I have usually found that "too busy" means "not interested." But under any circumstances, if the person does not want to talk with you, that is that. Several times, by the way, I have found that reluctant prospects will be less reluctant after a while, especially if they know I have talked to other people in the area. Try checking back with such sources from time to time in order to give them "progress reports," as it were. Sometimes that is all that is needed. Finally, there may be no question about the person having the information or not being willing enough to talk with you, but he or she may not be physically or mentally able to help you. If the person is very deaf, and you have a tendency to mumble, perhaps someone else should interview this prospect When I was gathering material on Larry Gorman, the subject of my first book, I went to see a man who, by all reports, had known Gorman well. He was glad enough to talk with me but too senile to be of much help; no matter what questions I asked, he would talk about whatever came into his head, which was never anything about Larry Gorman.

It is a good thing to remember—and all too easy to forget—that this decision-making is a two-way street, that the prospect is also deciding whether he or she wants to talk with you. After all, the whole business is an investment of time and energy on the prospect's part just as it is on yours, and once there is an agreement to go ahead you can be sure that it is based on a mutual feeling that there is something in it for each of you. You need not worry about this matter too much, but do spend a few moments looking at the situation from the prospect's point of view. It may be that the prospect feels he or she has something of value to tell both you and the world, in which case it would not be surprising if the prospect sought you out rather than the other way around. Several men have sent me lists of songs they knew, and one woman had her granddaughter come tell me that she was worried she was going to die and her songs would die with her. On the other hand, it may be that the prospect, pleased with the idea of being able to talk of the old days, has decided that you will be a good listener. It is difficult, sometimes, for a younger person to imagine the loneliness of old age and the release from it a series of interviews—meaning a series of visits—may represent. For some interviewees, the most important aspect of the interview is companionship, the simple joy of sharing a common space with another human being for even a little while. I am not, of course, suggesting that you interview someone because it will be good therapy, only that you take a moment to understand what a prospect's motivations may be, and, assuming they are honorable, do your best to accommodate them.

Such understanding may also help you deal with the prospects who are reluctant to be interviewed. They may feel that you will be using them, that you will make a lot of money out of this and where do they come in? If you are a student, you can answer such reluctance by explaining that you are working on an assignment or a paper. If you are not, you will simply have to offer the best explanation possible. I can say, however, that while I have found people who were quite incredulous about my taking all this trouble if I *was not* going to make something out of it, they simply accepted my story and that was that.

What, then, about prospects who want to be paid? I have heard of such requests, and should one arise I can offer a guideline, a reasonable exception, and a comforting thought. The guideline is, "Don't." The reasonable exception is that if someone has to take time off from gainful employment to talk with you, you should certainly offer compensation equivalent to what he or she would normally be making on the job. The comforting thought is that in over three decades of active fieldwork neither I nor my students have ever been asked for payment of any kind. On the other hand, you will often feel you want to do something for someone who has been especially helpful to you, and there is nothing wrong with that. Circumstances will suggest appropriate expressions of gratitude, but it is best to keep it on the level of what friends do for friends.

But if payment has not proved to be a problem, modesty has, and that brings us to consider a pretty basic matter. The layman's conception of history (and, sadly, that of too many historians) has been so conditioned by the "great man/significant event" approach that it is frequently difficult for an ordinary mortal to believe that anyone is really interested in unremarkable him. "Nothing important ever happened to me," says a man who worked in the lumberwoods all his long life. "I never did anything," says a woman who brought up a family of seven in a mill town on a mill hand's salary. Frequently this demurral is rather pro forma, the prospect needing only to be coaxed a little—and expecting to be. But occasionally it represents a sense of privacy or a conviction that life is something one lives, not talks about, so strong that you will not be able to overcome it. Naturally, if you encounter such convictions (and I have) you will have to accept them gracefully, no matter how senseless they seem. But this necessity does not arise very often. Usually, once the prospective interviewee understands that you really have not made a mistake, that you *are* interested in what he or she can tell you, you are set.

There is a corollary to the modesty problem: words come easily to some people, not so easily to others. Probably the first people you will be referred to will be the good talkers, the "character," who "knows a million of 'em," the man who "will talk your leg off." They may be fine sources, but if we believe in the non-elitist approach to art and history— and that is one of the things this manual is all about—should we depend on the loquacious only? The tape-recorded interview is the best technique we have ever had for reaching out into the great silences and making them articulate, but God forbid that we let the glib do all the talking! I am not recommending that we should seek out the dull or the half-witted; they are even more exceptional than the glib. Nor am I recommending that we should avoid the good talker. All I am saying is that if we are out to record some aspect of the lives of common men and women, we should be less concerned with whether prospects are articulate than with whether they have the experience we are interested in. If they have, there is a lot we can do to help them tell about it. But that is a subject for a later section.

When should you bring up the business of the tape recorder? If you are reasonably certain that the prospect will respond positively to the idea, you can bring it up in your initial letter when you explain all about what you are doing. The great advantage of this method is getting everything out in the open to begin with, and I am coming more and more to believe that it is a good plan. But since neither I nor my students have done this as a rule, I still offer my standard advice: wait until the end of the preliminary interview, especially if you feel that the prospect may be at all shy about it. Assure yourself that the prospect will be a good interviewee; make arrangements for your first interview; then bring up the tape recorder ("By the way, I'll be bringing a tape recorder. That way I won't have to bother you by taking notes all the time, and we'll be sure we get it right when I write it all down later on. O.K.?"). Very seldom will there be any serious objection that you cannot overcome with a little reassurance and gentle persuasion.

If, however, the prospect refuses to let you use the tape recorder, there is an alternative to calling the whole thing off. Make your appointment anyhow, and when you come to do the interview just start taking notes (bring the tape recorder with you but leave it out in the car). At some point, after some desperate note-taking and a few yelps like "Hold it" or "Would you repeat that again," request permission once more to use the tape recorder ("It'll be more accurate than my notes and a whole lot less bother for you," etc.). Sometimes this tactic works, and sometimes an interviewee may agree to let you use the tape recorder "next time." If the interviewee still refuses, though, and the refusal sounds final, you will have to decide whether it is worth continuing the series by taking notes and writing them up afterwards or whether it would be better to move on to work with someone else.

There will come a time when you will be tempted to record secretly, without the interviewee's knowledge or permission. It will be surprisingly easy to justify this action to yourself: the interviewee doesn't really "understand" how "important" this all is, you want to get the material "in its natural context," you don't want the tape recorder to "intrude" and spoil the "intimacy" of your conversation, etc.—all in the name of some high-sounding cause or entity like "scholarship." Learn early on to recognize the symptoms of this end-justifying-means distemper, and let your response be simple: *Don't do it.* It is an invasion of privacy, a betrayal of confidence, and a very shabby way for one human being to treat another.

As a corollary to the foregoing, always be sure the interviewee is aware of what is going to happen to the material you are gathering. Don't claim that the tape is simply something between the two of you and that it will be destroyed later on (unless, of course, that is literally true). Make it clear that the tapes will be preserved in an archives. If you find that this puts the interviewee off, try to determine what the problem is and offer reasonable assurances. We will have more to say about these assurances later, but for the moment don't make any promises neither you nor your archives can keep.

It is very helpful, both in your initial contact and in your preliminary interview, to mention how you came by the prospect's name ("I'm interested in lumber-camp cooking, and Charlie Dinsmore said you'd be a good person to talk to, because you'd cooked in the woods as far back as he could remember. . ."). The combination of credential and testimonial is a wonderful ice-breaker. Take advantage of it whenever you can.

There comes, finally, the question of whether a completely separate preliminary interview is always and absolutely necessary. Could you achieve the same results more efficiently over the phone? Yes, of course you could, especially if you already know the prospect or are working on familiar ground. And it is possible to combine the preliminary interview and the first interview ("Well, I've got the tape recorder right out in the car. What do you say we get started right now?"). I have done so frequently, especially when time is limited and I am working away from home. The sequence I have suggested—initial contact, preliminary interview, first interview—is simply a model I have found extremely workable, not only for myself but for my students as well, and as a model it can be adjusted to suit local circumstances, so long as the ground is covered and the spirit is fulfilled.

In sum, then, once you have determined that the prospect has the information you are looking for and that he or she is both willing and able to share it with you, you are ready to move ahead.

Advance Preparations

Before you go for your first interview, you should try to find out as much about your interviewee as you can. This does not mean that you should snoop or ask a lot of questions at the local store; I can think of no quicker way of getting off on the wrong foot. It simply means that you should check out obvious things like the feature article he mentioned that was written on his life in the local newspaper last year. If the interviewee has written a book, you should read it, especially if you are going to do more than just one or two interviews. If someone else has interviewed this person, check those interviews. All these things will keep you from asking questions that have already been thoroughly answered, save you time and money, and show the interviewee you are serious about what you are doing. I know from experience how deadly it can be to have interviewers ask questions that show they have never read a word I have written and how enlivening it can be when someone asks something like, "Now in the conclusion to *Joe Scott* you told how, etc. . . . Has that ever happened again?" Do your homework. It will pay off.

Do a little map work too, especially if you are unfamiliar with the areas you and your source will be talking about. What rivers are nearby? What lakes? What are the neighboring towns? A gas station road map is a big help, but if you want more detail, the U.S. Geological Survey ("Topographic") maps are excellent, giving the names of hills, coves, creeks, etc. You can purchase them at almost any good university bookstore and at many sporting goods stores too.) You need not commit *all* this detail to memory, but you will be surprised how much even a cursory knowledge of the lay of the land will help you.

If one of the things you will be talking about is some local event of more or less note, find out what you can about it ahead of time. A local history may give you a good summary of it; there may even be an easily available newspaper account. In addition, if you are going to be interviewing someone whose main experience was in some particular occupation, you should familiarize yourself as well as you can with the outlines and terminology of that occupation, not so that you can impress the interviewee with your wisdom but so that you will have at least some idea what he or she is talking about and some conception of what might be worth asking questions about. I remember one young girl, interviewing an old woodsman, who asked what they cut down the trees with. "Well, girlie," he said with a kind of amused contempt, "we used an ax, that's what we used!" Girlie looked him right in the eye: "Poll or double-bit?" she said. You could feel his attitude change. "Well, mostly poll axes, but later on. . . ." It comes down to this: The more you know about the interviewee's life, work, and times, the better equipped you will be to carry on the interviews—and the more you will enjoy your work!

Should you prepare a list of questions you want to ask? Unequivocally I say yes, but never let them get in your way in the interview itself. A list of questions, even a general list of subjects you intend to cover, will help immensely, especially if you are not an old hand at interviewing, just so long as you don't get locked into it by checking things off or reading directly from it. Part of your advance preparation should certainly be to plan what it is you hope to talk about, and even to note down some specific questions. More about this later on.

Take plenty of tape along with you, ideally brand-new tape. Few interviews go beyond a couple of hours, which is no more than you could get on one tape, but always take at least twice as much tape as you think you will need. And before you set out, take a moment to number a couple of tapes ahead of time. Write this number right on the cassette and on the box too, and include this number in all opening and closing announcements on the tape.

Use any numbering system that makes sense to you. You can simply number the tapes 1, 2, 3, . . . , or you can include the year (which is what I have always done: 80.1, 80.2, etc.). You can include the specific date (11/17/80 #1) or some combination of the interviewee's name, the date, and the number (Charlie 11/17/ #2). It doesn't matter how you do it, so long as you are consistent and the system makes sense to you (which assumes it will make sense to others). Of course, this number will go on your transcription too—one more simple way of keeping things straight. It will also help the archives staff later on, even though the archives will assign its own numbers to your tapes later. But don't try to use their system; in fact, it will avoid confusion if your system is clearly different.

Since you have now done your homework and know your equipment, you are all set to go, right? Wrong. Make a last minute check. Have you enough tape? Have you got the mike? (Did you leave it on your desk when you were "playing the game" last night?) Batteries? How about the plug-in cord (and, ideally, an extension cord)? Have you a pad and a pencil with an eraser (almost certainly you will need them)? Test your equipment just before you leave, because you may find that overnight, as W. C. Fields said, "Things happened!" I would suggest you test it by recording an advance announcement just before you set out. Let a good half-minute of tape go by blank, say twenty to thirty digits on the little counter (this will leave space for your archives to put its own identifying data on the cassette; then make an announcement modeled on the following: "This is Friday, September 29, 1980, and I am on my way to interview Mr. John O'Connor of Edinburg, Maine, about the days when he used to work on the Argyle Boom. My name is Thurlow Blankenship and this is my tape number 80.3." That is, give the date (and the *year*), the name and address of the interviewee, what (in a very general way) you plan to talk about, who you are, and the number of the tape. Now play it back. This will allow you to get some necessary information on the tape and check your equipment at the same time.

And so, as Dr. Williams said to his townspeople, "Go now / I think you are ready." Or as ready as you will ever be. Go on. It's going to be great.

The Diary or Journal

Of all the tasks required of a good fieldworker, I find that keeping a journal is the toughest. I come home from an interview, and either I am tired or I must get immediately to other things or—most likely—both; consequently, the journal doesn't get written. I have good journals for less than half of my fieldwork over the past thirty-five years, and I have had frequent occasion to regret that, because all too often the data I need when writing is just the sort of thing I would have put in my journal! But the fact that I have sinned and suffered the consequences makes me the ideal advocate for virtue: keep a journal, and keep it up to date.

It makes little difference what form you keep it in. I have found stiff-cover spiral notebooks workable, while I know one fieldworker who prefers to type his notes out and keep them in three-ring loose-leaf binders (his notes are absolutely a model of completeness too). I know others who are using laptop computers in the field. It may be that the archives where you will be depositing your tapes has specific require-ments of its own, and you can save yourself some trouble by inquiring ahead of time about this matter. Most likely, though, anything you turn in will be accepted. The two important things are to maintain the journal in a form that will make it easy for you to keep current and to have some con-sideration for whoever in years to come may wish to refer to it, which is to say keep it dated, clear as to persons and places, and legible.

What should go into the journal? In addition to the sort of informa-tion I have suggested in the preceding paragraph, you should enter almost any information that will help us appreciate what went on. Where does the interviewee live? Describe the neighborhood. Describe the home or the place where you conducted the interview. Were there many books around? Was there a rug on the floor? Pictures on the wall (and what kind of pic-tures)? Do you think he or she "got dressed up" for the occasion of the interview? Was anyone else around? What effect did their presence have on the interview? Did the interviewee seem to accept the tape recorder, or did he or she keep nervously glancing over at it? How were you feel-ing about the whole situation? Were you nervous? If you were ill or ex-cessively tired, say so. It might help a lot to know that there was a pic-ture on the wall that you found both fascinating and disturbing, and it would certainly help to know that you had the distinct feeling that at several points in the interview the interviewee was trying to get your goat. It is all but impossible to include too much, but as a guide for what to include or not include, simply ask yourself if this or that bit of infor-mation would help anyone listening to the tape or reading the transcript to make better use of it.

I have said that I am apt to get behind in this matter of keeping a journal. Lately, I have been trying a new technique: I keep a small cas-sette recorder with me. Then, while driving home from an interview, or immediately after I get home, I simply talk out my journal. Later, as soon as I have time, I transcribe the comments. In this way, since I am dictating while the experience is very fresh in my mind, my journals are more accurate and detailed. The only problem I foresaw was that I might never get around to transcribing my entries, but so far I have avoided that trap. And—most important—I am keeping up to date.

The Interview

Not only would it be pretentious for me to try and give a full treatise on interviewing here, it would be impossible. All I will do is give some technical advice that will help to make the recorded interview a more functional part of the whole process, and offer some suggestions on techniques I have used.

In order for the sort of interviewing we are concerned with to be as successful and useful as possible, there is a basic concept you should keep in mind: You are not holding a *dia*logue but always a *tria*logue, with the tape recorder itself as the third party. Too much interviewing is done with the dialogue structure in mind, the tape recorder being relegated to a kind of catch-as-catch-can eavesdropper role. The interview, for example, is held in a noisy restaurant, and the mike is simply placed on the table next to the sugar bowl. The resultant tape will be of some use to the interviewer as a kind of stenographic record of what went on, but it will not offer much to the rest of us. To be sure, there will be times when valuable information can be recorded only under extremely bad conditions, but nine times out of ten such conditions are avoidable. Think of the microphone as the representative of a number of people (transcribers, listeners, future scholars) who for one reason or another are extremely interested in what is being talked about; then treat it with the consideration its constituency deserves. Everything I have to say about such things as mike placement, announcements, testing, using photographs, and transcribing is based on this trialogue concept.

While no one should become overly concerned about it, your interviews will be much easier to listen to and transcribe if you can learn to reassure the interviewee that you are listening without continually saying "uh-huh" or its equivalent. Try simply nodding or smiling. The desirability of this silence on your part will be obvious when you come to transcribe your first interview, but while some will find it easy to keep quiet, others will find it almost impossible. It is not an important enough matter to insist on. It is merely one of those trialogue considerations, and it does help to be mindful of your own verbal tics.

In no sense should anything I have said be construed to mean that I consider the chief end of interviewing to be the making of beautiful tapes. That would require treating the tape recorder as the most important of the three participants in the discussion (more ridiculous than ignoring it completely, leading to such monstrosities as "Into the mike, please," or "Can't you speak more clearly, Mr. Jones?"). I do, however, believe that the recording should be as good as it can be under the circumstances, and the trialogue rather than the dialogue-cum-eavesdropper concept will work to that end.

That leads us to the formality/informality problem. Some people feel that the little formalities I have been and will be suggesting spoil the "intimacy" of the interview, working against the easy give-and-take of conversation and putting the interviewee on guard. There is something to that impression, but it is usually exaggerated, just as the idea that the introduction of a tape recorder into an interview will cause the interviewee to "freeze-up" is exaggerated (and such objections are usually raised by people with little or no experience in the actual situation). Informality is desirable, but the fact is that we are talking about an *interview*, not a conversation. You are gathering, and the interviewee providing, information to be processed and stored, and while you should certainly work to keep things relaxed and friendly, you are *not* simply "having a nice chat." You are doing a job of work, and the interviewee knows that just as well as you do. *You* won't forget that the tape recorder is there; don't expect the interviewee to (even if he or she is a good enough actor to evince surprise that "that thing's been going" all the time). And if your saying what will happen to the tapes puts people on guard, maybe they *should* be a little on guard. However, 94 percent of the time this "stiffening" will not become a problem. All will go easily, and you will wonder what the fuss was about.

I have already suggested that you test your equipment just before you leave home by putting an opening announcement on tape. I always do, but even so, I always repeat the announcement in the interviewee's presence, largely because it is a good ice-breaker. The interviewee and I will usually be chatting about something while I set up the machine, place the mike, and so on. Then, when I am ready to begin the interview, I pick the mike up and say something like, "Well, let's get started." Then I speak directly into the mike, not looking at the interviewee at all, while I say, "This is Friday, September 29, 1980, and I am up in Argyle, Maine, in the home of [*now I look up at the interviewee*] Ernest Kennedy, and we're going to be talking about the days when he was a river-driver. My name is Sandy Ives and this is my tape 80.3." Then I put the mike back in its place, sit back and relax, and continue: "O.K., now that's taken care of. Now. . . ." That is to say, I involve myself with the machine to begin with, then I involve the interviewee, and the interview is suddenly under way. I try to do it all in an offhand, diffident way. At the same time, I have made it unmistakably clear that the interview has begun.

From the outset, you should make certain that the interviewee understands what is going to happen to the tapes of the interview and that you get at least some acknowledgment of that understanding on the tape. From a strictly legal point of view, this acknowledgment has no value (that is, it does not constitute a "release"), but we at the Northeast Archives feel it shows our good intentions. You must tell the interviewees three basic things: that the tapes will be preserved, that people will be able to listen to them, and that they will be asked to sign a release at the end of the interview. I suggest some variation of the following, but try not to memorize it. Put it in your own words:

> I just want to tell you what's going to happen to these tapes we'll be making. They will be kept permanently in the Northeast Archives at the University of Maine. Then anyone who wants to find out how river-driving was done here on the Penobscot can learn by hearing about it from someone who actually did it himself. After the interview, I'll be asking you to sign a release, which will simply say that you're willing to have us use the material in this way. Is that O.K.?

If the interviewee has any questions or hesitations, now is the time to get them settled. If he or she wants to restrict the material somehow, you can explain whatever your archives' policy is in this regard and try to work out something satisfactory. But do not suggest the possibility of restrictions; let it come from the interviewee, if it comes at all.

There are two ways of getting the interviewee's acknowledgment on tape. First of all, you could simply explain the policy to him while the tape is running, just after you make your opening announcement. Or you could explain it all during your preliminary interview, or while you are setting up the tape recorder. If you do it this latter way, then all you need on the tape is something like, "O.K., now I explained about how we'll be keeping the tapes and about the release, didn't I?" and the interviewee's affirmative answer (or "silent consent").

You may want to check your equipment a few minutes into the interview. To that end, start off with something inconsequential and eminently interruptible, just to get the interviewee talking for a few sentences. This will give you a chance to check your VU meter for level. Once you think the settings are about right, you can just go ahead. But if you have any doubts about how your equipment is performing, you can simply say, "Excuse me, I just want to make sure this machine is working properly." Then rewind a little—just enough to tell you what you want to know—and play it back. Once you are satisfied, put the machine back in *record* mode and go ahead with the interview. (I italicize *record*, because I know of a case where the interviewer just said "O.K." and blithely completed the interview with the recorder in *play* mode. Believe me, that was one angry interviewer when he got home!).

Since tape has a way of running out just when you need it most, you should keep in mind that a C-60 cassette runs only thirty minutes to a side. Though an occasional glance at the cassette *should* be enough to tell you when to flip it over, I find it is often hard to see, especially when you're getting down toward the last ten minutes or so. Fortunately, some machines have a built-in pre-end alarm—it beeps or a light starts blinking when you get down to the last few minutes of tape. The point is, though, don't keep checking your watch, unless you've providentially set it down next to the recorder (a good idea, that). Any time you check your wrist, your interviewee will notice and be likely to conclude that you are either bored or in a hurry; it is a gesture that it is almost impossible to do gracefully. When it comes time to change, simply explain that fact, flip the cassette over, and make an announcement like the one with which you began, saying that this is a continuation of an interview, not the beginning of a new one.

Remember, a cassette only has two sides. When you flip it over, keep in mind that you have done so, and when you come to the end of the second side, *change cassettes*. It is very easy to accidentally start recording over on the first side, erasing the beginning of your interview or whatever you had recorded on side one. And when you get home and see what you've done, the self-anger and sense of stupid frustration you will feel will surpass even the time you locked the keys in the car! To guard against such a blunder, make sure the cassette sides are marked A and B, and always start with the A side.

How you conduct the interview will be largely a function of what it is you are looking for, and here I find it useful to distinguish between performance and discourse interviews. An example should make the point. Say the interviewee is a woman who has been recommended to you as knowing a lot of songs. Now a song is a discrete entity, having a very clear beginning, middle, and end. Frequently, you can even ask for one by name ("Can you sing 'Barbara Allen'?") or by type ("Do you know any other pirate songs?"), and the response will be the *performance* of a specific song. She will *sing* and you will listen, and—making allowance for the change of context—that is almost certainly the way the song would have been presented in its natural context (i.e. outside the interview context): a singer, a performer, presenting the item to an audience of sorts. By the time the interview is over, you will be able to say something like, "I collected twelve songs from Mrs. Callahan this afternoon."

Collecting "items" like songs or stories from people who are considered singers or storytellers (either by others or by themselves or both) is oftentimes a pretty easy business, once you have gotten them to agree to the idea in the first place—and frequently enough that is far from a hard thing to do. The interviewee knows very clearly what is expected—a series of performances—and all you have to do is sit quietly and listen like a good audience. Even if the interviewee is not an acknowledged performer, the situation will still be much the same. It may be a little more difficult to get such a person to perform ("I never was much of a singer"), but once it is clear you are looking for specific *items* he or she knows ("—but my father was a real singer, and I guess I heard most of them often enough so I know them—"), you are well on your way ("—and I guess I could sing 'em for you somehow."). The interview will still be a series of performances.

You will recall that I described the interview situation as a trialogue. In the performance-oriented interview, the interviewee will be performing for both you and the tape recorder. You as interviewer will have a triple role. During the performances you will be the attentive, extremely attentive, audience; between performances you will be a kind of low-key master of ceremonies; and all the time you will be a sound engineer, paying considerable attention to both the equipment and the ambience, which is to say that the tape recorder itself will assume considerable importance. You may do "test takes" and spend time monitoring the performance through earphones or fussing with exact mike placements (you may even bring in specialized equipment like mike booms). If there are other people in the room, you may even find yourself "hushing" them. In brief, roles will be very clear. The recording of performances makes perfect sense all around. In fact, it seems as though that is what one *ought* to be recording.

On the other hand, rather than looking for specific items, you may be more interested in a way of life, a process, an occupation, or some historical or legendary event or person. You may simply want to interview someone with nothing more specific in mind than getting a life history of the most rambling sort, either for its own sake or with an eye to editing it all into a biography some day. What is important is not performance but *discourse* and the information carried by that discourse, and the roles of the three trialogue participants will be quite different from what they would be for a performance-oriented interview. As the interviewer, you will be asking questions and actively eliciting information from the interviewee, who will be responding to your leads (at least in part). You will want to encourage the easy flow of information, and while some formality is inevitable and even desirable (as I said earlier, you are *not* just having a nice chat), you should do everything you can to keep the interviewee from feeling he is "on stage." To this end, you should pay as little attention as possible to the tape recorder and the mike, after seeing that both are well and unobtrusively placed, and you will be less concerned with maintaining an acoustically perfect ambience (hushing people, fretting when the telephone rings, etc.). In fact, if newcomers do interrupt the interview, you can take it as some indication that you have been successful in keeping it low-key and easy. They will not be embarrassed until they see the recorder. After all, a simple conversation seems like the sort of thing one ought *not* to be recording.

This is not to say that specific items of folklore will not surface in such interviews. They will crop up frequently, but still in the context of the general discussion. The interviewee may use proverbial comparisons ("That man was tougher'n a bag of hammers") or tell a joke ("Course that's like the two Irishmen was walking down the street and . . .") to illustrate a point. (By the way, some of the best examples of traditional remedies I have ever collected have come to me in this way: "That ax jumped off that knot and cut my shin clean to the bone, but I just put some tobacco on it, and it healed all right.") The interviewee may also respond to your requests for specific items ("Well that was old Archie Stackhouse, and the way I heard it was he. . ."). The point is, though, that the material does not come to you as performance but as information. The interviewee may, in your opinion or in the opinion of others, be a good talker or even a "good storyteller," but the stories do not come for their own sake but rather as illustrations of a point or in response to a question. The specific items are not the important matter; the information they carry is.

Having made this distinction between performance and discourse, let me hasten to say that practically never will an interview be made up of one or the other exclusively. They are not polarities but rather the limits of a continuum, and any interview will contain elements of both. Ballad-singing is about as pure performance as you are apt to come across, yet in a song-collecting interview there probably will be some discussion between the songs. On the other hand, the proverb is a very discursive or conversational genre, yet by the very fact that it calls attention to itself and the speaker it is to some extent performed. While most of the users of this manual will be conducting discursive interviews, there are very few folklorists who have not put in some time recording straight performances. Keeping the performance/discourse distinction in mind should help you understand what is going on in a particular interview and how you should behave in order to keep it going.[5]

One final word on performance interviews is in order here. Since you will be playing the audience role, try to determine what the performer expects of an audience. For example, I have found that in Maine and the Maritimes, singers are sometimes put off by people who appear to be listening too intently ("She just kept staring at me!"), who "relate" to the song too obviously (by swaying their bodies, smiling sincerely), or who join in on the refrains. Yet if a man falters, I have found it is all right (especially in Irish communities) to say something like "Good for you, John." Generally, though, one sits there, silent, reserved, maybe looking at the floor, maybe not. It took me some time to learn the role, but I am awfully glad I did.

It may be helpful to keep yet another distinction in mind. Kenneth Goldstein distinguishes between natural and artificial contexts in folklore.[6] Here, there are essentially three criteria involved. In a natural context, the song or tale is presented *by* someone who would normally perform it, *for* people who would be the usual audience, and *at* a time and place when such performance would be expected. Any other context is an artificial one. The ideal, of course, is to study folklore in its natural context. For example, if you are studying children's games, you can simply spend a lot of time watching children at play from some vantage point where your presence will not disturb them or affect their actions. In this way you will see the games in their completely natural context. Should you make yourself obvious (for instance, by standing nearby and taking notes or using a tape recorder or camera), you can be almost certain that your presence will affect what is going on, and the context will therefore be to some extent artificial. If you move off the playground completely and spend your time interviewing children about what games they play, you will be operating in a still more artificial context, and if you interview adults about games they used to play when they were children, you will have gone one step further.

Obviously, the techniques discussed in this manual are entirely aimed at collecting in an artificial context. My own work is a perfect case-in-point. I have written extensively on lumbercamp songs, yet I have never

lived in a lumbercamp nor heard an old come-all-ye sung along the dea-
con seat. All my collecting has been done from men who *had* been woodsmen themselves and *used* to sing these songs in camp or *remembered*
hearing them sung there. And the interviews were conducted years after the fact, in kitchens and parlors all over the Northeast. Clearly, then,
I have had to rely on material gathered outside its natural context.

Yet the artificial context may be the only one in which you *can* gather
your data, because the natural context no longer exists (there are, for instance, no more all-winter lumbercamps). In such a situation, you can re-
construct the natural context by asking all sorts of questions about, say,
what life was like in an all-winter lumbercamp, when singing took place,
who sang, who listened, and so forth. Even if you can still gather data
in its natural context, there will always be supplementary material that
can be best covered in a follow-up interview. Say, for instance, you
have recorded a country/western singer's performance at a local bar—
certainly a natural context.[7] The next day you go to his home, interview
him in his living room, and, in the process, get him to sing over several
of the songs he sang the night before. Obviously, then, the interview
context is by its very nature an artificial one, yet there is nothing wrong
with that, so long as you don't fool yourself or attempt to fool others
about what it is you are doing or have done. Anyone who makes pronouncements about a form he or she has never observed in its natural
context must understand the limitations of these pronouncements and
make those limitations clear to readers.

As the interview moves along, keep this rule in mind: *The tape should
be as complete and accurate a record of the interview as you can possibly make
it.* Remember that a tape recording has no visual aspect, and many things
that will be clear to you, since you were there at the time, will not be
clear to someone else who was not there. (Chances are they will not
even be clear to *you* some years, months, or even days later.) Keep the
trialogue concept in mind, thinking of the tape recorder as the *blind*
third party, for whom all gestures, pointings, and the like must be in-
terpreted. In this way, some of the visual material can be captured right
on the tape. If someone gestures that something was "about that long,"
you can say, "About three feet, eh?" Or if he says, "He was over there,
and I was right here," drawing it out in the air for you, you can interject
somewhere, "That'd be about fifty yards away on your left, then?" Still,
such gesturing frequently becomes a problem when someone is explaining how to do something like notching a log or building a cabin. Occasionally, you can get the interviewee to draw a picture for you (one reason why you should always have paper and pencil at hand), or you can

draw it out and ask, "Is this the way you mean?" Then you can include these drawings as part of your transcription, indicating in the text just where the drawing comes into play (for example, [*See drawing no. 1*]). You can sometimes explain extraneous noises right on the tape, too ("Wow, that jet sounded awful low" . . . "Is that a chain saw out there?"), but at the very least you should explain all such matters in your transcript.

If you feel that what is being conveyed by gesture is crucial, don't hesitate to slow the interview down to the point where you can interpret the gestures properly ("Now whoa, let's see now, there were three of those piers maybe fifty feet apart standing in a line out from shore and you say you were standing halfway between the second and third?"). It is very likely that at moments like this the interviewee will be looking for reassurances from you by saying "Y'see?" or "Know what I mean?" more often than usual, and you should steel yourself against giving such reassurances when you really do *not* "see" or when you know the explanation will not be clear to the tape recorder. But sometimes it is all but impossible to slow things down, in which case make a note to yourself to write out—using your own words and diagrams—a good description of the process in question and then ask about it in a subsequent interview. This technique will give the interviewee a chance either to approve or to correct your description, which will go a long way toward clarification.

It may be that a tape recording can in no way convey the process in question, or can only do so at the price of fantastic verbal contortions on your part, while a movie, a videotape, or even a series of still photographs could do the job very simply. It might be barely possible, for instance, to describe a series of dance steps in words, but it would be much more worthwhile to get a good videotape of the same steps. Showing such a videotape and then taping the interviewee's comments might be extremely valuable, just as a description of a whittled object would be made more valuable by some accompanying photographs. But the incorporation of visual aids into an interview raises its own problems, which we will take up at a later time.

As a rule, you should keep the tape running throughout the entire interview. Don't turn it on and off to "save tape" or to avoid recording material that seems "irrelevant." For one thing, you may not be a very good judge of what is irrelevant or unimportant. Besides, such on-the-spot editorializing can be insulting. The person you are talking to may feel that what you are being told is very relevant and important, and no matter how bright and politely interested you manage to look, your killing the machine will be noticed. Then, when something you think is important comes up again, you will miss recording the beginning—and that may be very important. It is simplest, politest, and generally best just to leave the tape running and not get involved in this kind of judgment.

On the other hand, there will certainly be times when you should turn the machine off temporarily. If the interviewee is called out of the room for a minute to answer the phone, or some such matter, or if company arrives and all attention is turned that way for a while, it makes sense to stop recording. Sometimes you can get an explanation of the interruption right on the tape ("Mr. O'Connor has to go outside and talk to a delivery man, so I'm shutting down for a minute"), or you can enter it in your transcript later on, along with a statement of about how long the tape was off. Then when you begin again, you can simply mention what the interviewee's last remarks were and continue.

What do you do when you are told to "shut the damn thing off for a minute"? The answer is simple: *shut it off.* Don't spend time trying to get permission to leave it running, and certainly never play tricks like leaving it on when you say you have turned it off. Confidence and trust are too important to be trifled with, and you should do nothing that might make interviewees unsure either of you or of their own judgment. This is especially true if you are a stranger. Turn the machine off—quickly, calmly, and cheerfully. It may be that what you are told off the record is material you would just as soon leave off the record. That is the way it will work out most of the time, which means there is no real problem and you are both glad the tape was stopped. But if the material is something you *are* interested in, you *do* have a problem, and it will require tact to solve it.

The chances are that it will become perfectly obvious why you were asked to turn the machine off. The interviewee may even volunteer the reason, or you can ask. In any event, there are two classic explanations for reluctance of the "turn-that-thing-off" variety: the material in question is felt to be either inappropriate or threatening.

Interviewees may be concerned that a story is "too foolish" to go on the tape, or that it has "nothing to do with what we're talking about," or (and this is a very common concern) that it is "off-color." In a sense, then, they are trying to be considerate and not waste your tape, which leaves it up to you to convince them that the material is anything *but* foolish or irrelevant. I have sometimes found that this reluctance is not only very superficial, it is a feint on the interviewee's part to determine whether I really want "that sort of thing" (it frequently works this way in connection with off-color material). Sometimes you can spot this tactic ahead of time. I remember one man who, having just sung me seven or eight wonderful old ballads, suddenly chuckled and said that "maybe we better not put this one on." I sensed the feint and encouraged him to go ahead, which he did. The song was riotously funny, but, since he had been singing serious ballads all afternoon, he wanted assurance that I would not object to "such a foolish thing."

It may be, however, that the reluctance has deeper roots, such as not wishing to speak ill of the dead or fearing that whatever is said will "get back" to the person under discussion or his family. The interviewee may fear (rightly or wrongly) getting involved in libel or slander or may simply not be sure enough of the information to want to go on record about it. In these situations you must find a way to allay those concerns (assuming, of course, that you do not share them). Don't hurry the situation. Make a mental note of the material, and come back to it later. I would even recommend waiting until a subsequent interview; it is surprising how reluctance fades as the interviewee comes to know and trust you. Even so, you may still have to offer some encouragement by explaining why this is just the sort of material you need, that it will not get back to or harm anyone, and so forth. You may even offer (if it seems necessary, and if your archives is willing) to restrict the material in some suitable way. Here you will have to use your judgment, but remember two things. First, never offer well-meaning assurances you cannot make good on. Second, do not commit either yourself or your archives to imposing restrictions on an interview that are patently in excess of what is needed simply to allay someone's concern over possible repercussions. The offer of restrictions should come as a last resort.

Who is "in charge" of the interview? Who controls the direction it takes? Since you know what it is you want to find out, the simplest answer is that you are the one who will guide it, but it doesn't always work that way, nor should it. At the beginning, assume that you are going to direct the interview, but interviewees may have ideas of their own of what they want to talk about. Be conscious of what is happening, and listen carefully. They may seem to get off on terrible tangents, but they may also be telling you about what they know best, and you should explore those things first. For example, I remember one ex-woodsman who led the discussion into the business of being a teamster, which obviously interested and excited him. The interviewer listened politely, then said, "Uh, yes, now I was asking you what the different buildings were in a camp. Would you. . . ." She put the interview back where she wanted it and got answers to her questions, but the fire was out. Even his discussion of teaming in a later interview was less spirited. She should have gone with him and explored the teamster business when he wanted to talk about it and then come back to other matters later. So when it comes to the question of directing the interview, the answer is that you should, but be ready to let go intelligently.

There is another good reason for not being too insistent about directing the interview: sometimes the sequence in which subjects come up may be particularly revealing. A shift in subject, a sudden (or not so sudden) tangent—what brought it about? What suggested it? You ask about one thing and you get another: why? If, for example, you try to hold to a neat chronological sequence and the interviewee keeps breaking out of it, rather than becoming exasperated at this disorderliness, try asking yourself what order he or she might be following. I warn you against cheap psychologizing, but associations, avoidances, and substitutions can give you valuable information. Once again, it is a matter of letting go intelligently and (without insisting on an insight in every tangent) listening carefully.

Earlier on, I recommended the use of lists of topics you want to cover and questions you want to ask. It may be that you can pick up ready-made interview guides or questionnaires from your archives or from the project you are working on. There are several state guides available. Then there are the vast compendia like the Irish *A Handbook of Irish Folklore* and the British *Notes and Queries on Anthropology* (see the Bibliography), but none of these works will be any substitute for your own knowledge of your field of inquiry, especially your knowledge of what areas are not well known and need documentation. Never ask a question you do not understand yourself. That sounds self-evident, but it is one of the traps someone else's list of questions can lead you into. For instance, you should never ask a question such as, "Did you ever use a— a parbuckle—to yard logs?" when you don't even know what a yard is. Your interviewee will not be fooled, and you will just be confused and bored by his answers. This is not to say that you have to be an expert or that you should only ask questions to which you already have the answers. There will be many things that will not be clear to you, and you should certainly ask questions about them, but that is a different matter from not even understanding what the question itself means. The best advice I can give on interview guides and pre-prepared questionnaires is that you should use them ahead of time to help you prepare your own list of questions. The very act of compiling such a list will help to fix the questions in your mind, *and that is where they should be.*

The second best bit of advice I can offer about using an interview guide is that you should be extremely careful about getting tied to it or excessively dependent upon it. Again, don't read questions from it; pay no attention to it while the interviewee is talking (never leaf through it

or check things off), and don't for heaven's sake let it take over the interview by becoming in your mind something to be "gotten through."
You should not even consider getting through it a virtue!

Once you have the formalities of the opening announcements and
the explanation of what will happen to the tapes out of the way, how
do you get the interview itself started? A great deal will depend on what
it is you are looking for and what the interviewee's expectations may be
(what you said in your letter, what was discussed in the preliminaries,
etc.). You will always have a reason for setting up an interview; we can
take that for granted, but it may be a pretty vague or general reason. You
may have an interest in logging and lumbering, and an interviewee who
spent many years of his life as a woodsman, or you may be interviewing
a woman to find out what it was like to spend fifty years as a farm wife
in northern Aroostook County. Frequently you will be interested not
in someone's whole life but in some specific segment of it, such as the
year a woman might have spent as district nurse before her marriage, or
what it might have been like to work in a cotton mill during the years
the union was trying to get established there. The last of these is by far
the most specific topic, but even so we can still describe it as a general area
for questioning rather than a specific question. And the same would hold
true if you were interviewing someone recommended as a great storyteller
or singer of old songs.

I can suggest a model for getting started, so long as we understand
it to be nothing more than a model: begin general, become specific.
Start by getting the basic biographical information, if that comes easily—age, place of birth, family, schooling, length of residence here and
elsewhere, etc.—but don't insist on anything. These are useful ice-
breaking questions, but if you find the interviewee becoming restive,
move on to something else. Move into the list of possible questions you
have made up, but be very alert to what it is he or she may want to talk
about, and try to follow those leads wherever possible. In the beginning,
it is just as important (perhaps even crucial) to show interviewees that
you are interested in them and the things they are interested in as it is
to gather data. Call it a combination of "establishing rapport" and ex-
ploring, because it certainly is both. Let your interviews move, then,
from the general and non-directed, with special attention to establishing rapport, to the controlled and specific, with continued attention to
maintaining that rapport.

There is an exception to this approach that, on the one hand, is a
very large one and, on the other, is not really an exception at all. If you
have come to interview someone in regard to something very specific,

don't waste a lot of time on generalities. Get right to it, especially if the interviewee knows why you have come, largely because it is the most natural thing to do. As a matter of fact, some of the best interviews I have ever conducted, and certainly some of the best interviews my students have conducted, have come about when we stood the foregoing model on its head. In this connection, it is time to talk about the principle of serendipity.

I have always found that fieldworkers (especially novice fieldworkers) do their best work when looking for something very specific, and frequently the more specific it is the better. I would never turn a student loose to go look for "folklore" or even "information" on old times. I would insist on a sharper focus, say "the fire of 1910," or "Old Dalton and his stories," or "bears and bear hunting," or "the Collins murder," and I recommend the same approach to readers of this manual. Such focusing is especially useful if you are working with virtual strangers in a strange area, because it gets the interview off to a good solid start: the interviewee knows what you are looking for, and you know what you want to ask. But (and here is the serendipity) as the interview progresses, keep your mind open for material you could not have known enough to ask for and may not even have dreamed existed.

Serendipity is the story of my life. While I was trying to learn all I could about songs of the Maine lumberwoods, I first heard of Larry Gorman. While I was interviewing a man about Gorman, he told me about Joe Scott. And while I was gathering material for my book on Scott, I had a man tell me about Lawrence Doyle.[8] Two years later, a man I was interviewing about Doyle turned out to be a creditable fiddler and also introduced me to a whole cycle of tall tales told by and about yet another local character. At another time I had gone to collect songs from a man who had been described to me as a fine singer (he was, too), when a chance visitor happened to mention the name of a local poacher, about whom the singer proceeded to tell several stories (that poacher became the subject of another book!). In each case I was looking for one thing; in each case I found something of value I had not expected. I could offer further examples, and I am sure other folklorists could easily duplicate my experience, but the point is made: know what you are looking for and go for it, but never let yourself be blind to other possibilities. The most interesting material of all may turn out to be what you catch out of the corner of your eye. This is the principle of serendipity, and it will always work in your favor, if you let it.

It is obvious why this approach *is* an exception to the general-to-specific model. But at the same time it is *not* an exception because it uses the specific search largely as an opener, a way in. Once you get beyond it, you are back to the model again in a very easy and natural way. When my students and I were compiling material for our book on Argyle Boom (see the bibliography at the back of this book), we had several interviews with Ernest Kennedy, who had sorted and rafted logs there for years. Some time after the project was completed, I was going over the catalogs of our interviews with Ernest and saw all kinds of little suggestions of further riches ("That was the spring after I came back from Allagash," . . . "I was cooking that winter for my father up on Hemlock Stream. . . ," etc.). I went back to see him and ultimately had at least forty hours of interview with him.

So much depends on who you are, whom you are interviewing, and the particular chemistry of your interaction, that is almost impossible to give specific advice on how to conduct an interview once you have made your beginning. Some people are self-starters, talk easily, give lots of detail, move from one subject to another effortlessly, and in general need very little help from you, although you may want to keep the tangents from becoming too tangential. Others will require more work on your part, because for one reason or another they will not volunteer much. Such a person may know a lot and have a great fund of experience but find the words hard to come by. What can you do to help?

First, you can help by creating as easy and relaxed an atmosphere for the interview as is possible under the circumstances. Second, you can help by showing that you really are interested in what the interviewee has to say and that you recognize its importance. My third suggestion is that you help with the kinds of questions you ask. One of the classic bits of advice is never to ask a question that can be answered by yes or no. It is good advice, but I find it devilishly hard to follow (Q: "Did you ever drive team?" A: "Sure") and not always that much of a problem so long as I remember to follow up (Q: "Where was that?" A: "Well, . . ."). That leads me to my fourth and most important suggestion: *probe.*

A probe is simply a device for eliciting more and better information in an interview, or, to put it another way, of helping the interviewee tell a story more completely. For example, among the kinds of answers you will get to your opening questions, especially in interviews on occupations, is what I call the "they" answer. You ask, "How would you go about building a road in the woods?" and the answer comes, "Well, the first thing they'd do would be to . . ." or "Well, first you'd. . . ." Now there is nothing really wrong with that sort of answer; in fact you will get some excellent descriptions of tasks and processes in this form, because it is a very natural way to describe things. (As a matter of fact, it is probably the way *you* would describe a process you were familiar with yourself.) But when you are interviewing, do not let description stop there. Get interviewees to describe their own particular and unique experiences with these tasks or processes.

Raymond Gorden's good book deals with the matter of probes at great length, and what I have to say will be much simpler and less systematic."[9] But if your interviewee has given you a good "they" answer, you can often get particulars by asking such questions as the following:

> Did that ever happen to you?
> Did you ever do that yourself?
> Can you give me an example of that?
> Where was this? When?
> Wait a minute. I don't quite see how that worked. Now you say
> that. . . .

Sometimes a simple evincing of surprise will serve as a probe ("That many?" "Were they as big as all that?"), or a quizzical look or raised eyebrow may be enough.

One of the most effective probes—and it is a good deal more than that—is simple *silence*. Don't be afraid of silence, first of all; never feel that you have to keep talking. Try shutting up and see what happens. Learn to interpret whether a pause means that the interviewee has really finished and is waiting for guidance from you or is only considering what to say next. Take your time in either case. Jump in too quickly and you may head off further useful details or an interesting if serendipitous shift in subject. Remember that the interviewee will be just as conscious of the silence as you are, and just as anxious to fill it). This is not to say there cannot—and will not—be *awkward* silences; it is just to say that silence can be useful.

Another valuable kind of probe is the question based on something said in an earlier interview ("Last time I was here you mentioned that, during the winter you worked up around Kennebago, you were on a hot yard. Now I'm not clear just what a *hot* yard was. Could you go into that a little for me?"). There are any number of things you can do with this sort of retrospective probe, like finding out where or when something took place, getting more details, or checking previous ones. It is an excellent kind of question because, among other things, it shows that you have been paying attention to what he said and are really serious about your work. Conversely, nothing can alienate someone like making him or her go over the same ground again out of mere forgetfulness.

On the other hand, there are times when you *should* get the same story more than once. Frequently, for instance, people have stories they tell about themselves that have become pretty much "set pieces." That is, they have told them so often that they have become quite fixed in their structure and details. Such stories are often among the first to be told, or they may have developed "titles" (a friend may say, "Get him to tell you about the time the skunk got in the furnace"). At any rate, however you come to recognize such material, it is an excellent idea to get that story two, three or even several times. Perhaps you could take a friend along and ask that it be told to him or her, but usually it is no problem to get a favorite story repeated.

I cannot overemphasize the importance of recording the same item more than once. Someone singing a song for you may leave a stanza out—accidentally or on purpose—yet cover the omission so smoothly that you have no way of knowing it took place. Repeated singings on different occasions could reveal such omissions. Conversely, something that sounds like a mistake the first time through may turn out to be quite purposeful. There may be several ways of telling the same story depending on who it is being told for, where it is being told, when, etc. Naturally, all of us like to gather "new" material, and it is understandable if you chafe when the interviewee comes up with "that damn skunk story" again. But if you are interested in oral tradition—if you're a folklorist, of course you are; if you're an oral historian, you should be!—you must learn not only to accept repetition gracefully but even to seek it out on occasion.

By the way, this re-eliciting is also valuable for checking facts. In two different descriptions of an experience, do the names stay the same? Are the same numbers involved? Where did it take place? When? This process is not so much to see whether someone is telling the truth (though it can help determine that, if you have some doubts) as it is to discover what is important and what is not. For example, I had a man tell me about someone coming back from the dead as a big white dog to drive off some land speculators who were annoying his wife. The next time the man told the story, it involved a black dog. That variation does not invalidate his story; it just means that the color was an inconsequential detail for him.

How about "leading questions"? Some people call them "loaded questions," but whatever you call them they are questions in which you put words into someone's mouth by framing your question in such a way that the response you want is perfectly clear. A gentleman who will be happier nameless was interviewing an elderly Micmac Indian, and the Indian told him something that had happened years ago. "Don't you think," said the interviewer, "that is a good example of the way the white man has exploited the Indian all these years?" "Yes sir!" came the reply, "it sure is." Stay away from that sort of futile exercise. It is tempting, and it makes you feel as though you are getting somewhere, but the results are worse than useless because they are misleading.

On the other hand, there is one kind of leading question I have used with considerable success: the *negative* leading question. I have found it especially useful in gathering biographical information, not about the interviewee but about some third party. If you ask, "What kind of a guy was he?" (and by the way that is still a perfectly decent way to begin, but listen very carefully to what is said and not said), you will probably be told that he was a pretty nice fellow. If you ask, "Was he a good man?" you will probably be told that he was indeed a good man. But if you come at it negatively, you can get interesting results. For example, while I was gathering material for my biography of the songmaker Joe Scott, I wanted to see how one interviewee who knew him well would react to a negative assessment of Joe's character, "Look," I said, "I was talking to someone the other day, and he told me that Joe was just a damn nuisance around the camps." No one, in fact, had told me any such thing, but if my interviewee agreed with that assessment, he could say so without feeling that he had been the one to bring it up. If he did not agree, he would find it very easy to say so, and that is just what he did, vehemently. "No sir!" he said, and went on from there. You need not always invent such opinions, either. I knew that one man I was writing about had the reputation of being a thief. One interviewee telling me a lot about him was carefully avoiding that side of the story, until I remarked, "Couple of people told me he would have been a real fine guy but he couldn't stop stealing stuff." The reply came slowly, but smilingly: "Well, I wasn't going to say anything about that, but if you already know about it, yes. . . ." Be judicious with the negative leading question. Use it only after you have used more standard methods, but it will sometimes stir things up just the right way.

The length of the interview will vary with each interviewee. I have gone on for several hours, and I have quit after ten minutes, depending upon whom I was talking to and what I was looking for. Still, I would offer this as a pretty good rule of thumb: one hour, give or take a little. It is not only that the interviewee may become tired; you will too, and an hour is about all either of you will want. You can always go back again, of course. In fact, you probably will be going back several times, and it is always better to stop too soon than to risk wearing out your welcome. But say transportation is a problem. You have traveled a hundred miles to see someone, and at the end of an hour you have just begun. Use your own judgment, but you might consider taking a break ("Look, we've been going at this for about an hour now, and I should go downtown and do a few errands, so why don't I come back after supper?"). That will give you a chance at least to listen to the interview so far and formulate some questions based on it.

Another small formality. Make a closing announcement at the end of the interview similar to your opening one: "This is the end of the interview with Ernest Kennedy, Argyle, Maine, by Sandy Ives, September 29, 1980." Sometimes I do this right at the interview, sometimes I wait until later. It doesn't matter, but it should be there just to close things out.

How many interviews should you hold? Frequently you will need only one, but I have had as many as twenty, and others have gone well beyond that. The more I work at this game, though, the more I see a sort of minimum unit: *one interview and a follow-up*, which is to say two interviews. As I review my work, I find occasions where in my haste I neglected to have a follow-up interview, and almost every time I have had leisure to regret it. I find something I should have asked, something that needed clarification or amplification, but by then it is too late. That is why I suggest you should consider the follow-up interview as routine, and you should also consider it routine to review the first interview with some care before the follow-up. It would be ideal if you could have the transcript completed, but that is not always possible. However you review your interview, take careful notes on questions you want to ask. Thus, the minimum requirement for good technique involves four steps: advance preparation, the interview itself, a review of that interview, and a follow-up. If that leads to more interviews, fine; if it does not, you have a good solid document nonetheless.

If you think it was tough getting started, wait until you try to conclude a series of interviews. You may find that you have come to know the interviewee rather well, and now you both face the prospect of not seeing each other again. I will not presume to tell you how to proceed in such a personal matter, beyond making one suggestion: Don't hold out the promise of continued friendship and future visits, unless you are very sure you can keep that promise. In theory, I can say it is better to keep the whole thing limited from the start by maintaining a sort of semibusiness arrangement. If you see that one more session ought to clean things up, you can say something like, "I think I've got about another hour's worth of questions, so why don't I plan to come back once more next week for a sort of wrap-up?" I say "in theory," because that is much easier for me to suggest than it has been for me to do, and at the last moment I have blurted out, "Oh, I'll be back one of these days," when I was not at all sure I would be. The fact is, though, I have been lucky and made good on that promise more often than not. I have formed some lasting friendships through my fieldwork. There are many towns in Maine and the Maritimes I wouldn't think of driving through without stopping to have a "shake-hands" with Edmund or Art or Jim or (as it happens more and more) driving out to the churchyard to stand a minute by their graves. As I say, I have been lucky. How you handle this problem is up to you, of course; just don't ignore it. And when you are through, write a thank-you letter.

Interviewing with a Camcorder

Since this is essentially a book on audio recording, I'm rather assuming that the idea of using video will come up because you happen to have a camcorder available. Given my limited experience with this device, I won't offer advice on equipment, but I believe I can make some suggestions on its use that will help to keep a perfectly good idea from becoming an embarrassment.

Over the past decade, camcorders have become almost as common as cassette recorders. They are extremely easy to use under all kinds of light conditions ("point-and-shoot" describes them well), they can run for up to two hours on a single cassette, their cost is competitive with the better audio machines, and—even in the hands of the most egregious of amateurs—their results are nothing short of remarkable. Minute for minute videocassettes cost no more than good audiocassettes, and they are certainly less expensive than color film (let alone black-and-white!). In short, the camcorder is the gadget supreme, offering instant expertise and excellent results. The only major problem seems to be that found with digital audio: the signal deteriorates rapidly, but we can assume that that problem will be solved in due time.

It would seem logical, then, that video interviewing would simply take over from audio interviewing, and I have already pointed out a couple of places where its judicious use would make all the difference—in documenting crafts or work techniques, for example. I can see it being used in on-site interviews, too. The question is, though, how advantageous is it for the straight one-on-one interview that is the main subject of this book, and here my opinion wavers between "not much but maybe some" and "maybe some but not much." With my demonstrated (if naive) faith in technology and my all-American love of gadgets, how can I be so tepid? It's just that I haven't found the visual information adds enough to what the audio alone would have delivered to make it worth the extra trouble and expense.

One problem I have found with camcorded interviews is the same one I find with many slide/tape productions I have seen: the pictures are beautiful, the sound so-so. With slide/tape shows that is sometimes not so bad, because the slides are apt to be the more important part, but in an interview the main message is obviously going to be carried by the audio. Therefore, if you use a camcorder, pay especial attention to getting good sound. Unfortunately, all the camcorders I know of have automatic level control *only*, and while the built-in mike is usually adequate, obviously you cannot get it as close to the interviewee as it should be. Most (but not all) have a jack that will allow you employ an external mike, and everything I've had to say up to now about mike placement and the like goes double when you're using a camcorder. Clip-on mikes are ideal, and don't make a big thing out of hiding the wire (one of my students uses a wireless mike with good results, by the way).

Another problem is the temptation to make a production out of what should be a rather straightforward record. Keep all zooming, cutting away and panning to a minimum, and concentrate on the business at hand, which is the interviewee and what he or she has to say. Not that you shouldn't take advantage of the camera's ability to record ambience; in fact I recommend that you take shots of the neighborhood, the house, the room where the interview will take place, who else is there, etc. But once the interview itself is under way, set the camera where it will show the interviewee best and for the most part leave it there. If the interviewee gestures a great deal or is demonstrating something, you will want to shoot from far enough away to include that action in your frame—and here comes an exception to my rule: in a demonstration, there might well be good reason to zoom in to show just the hands holding the tool or object. But take it easy; what seems like a reasonable breaking-up of the tedium while you're shooting will often look like frantic swooping and switching when you play it back. And that will detract from the tape's value as a record of what went on.

There are two possible shooting formats that I have seen used successfully in one-on-one interviews: over-the-camera and on-camera. Interviewing over-the-camera is the one that I have seen used most often.

The interviewer asks questions from behind or next to the camera, and the interviewee alone is on the screen, appearing to speak directly to the camera. It is sometimes disparagingly called the "talking head" format, but it is very common—we see it all the time on television—and it gets the job done. If you are going to use it, I recommend a tripod, and spend a little extra money to get a sturdy one, since any movement of the camera is apt to be magnified many times in playback, especially if you have the zoom extended.

In the on-camera format, both the interviewer and interviewee appear on the screen, the interviewer having set the camera up and started it rolling ahead of time. I suppose there are any number of ways to arrange the "set," but the best I ever saw simply had interviewer and interviewee facing each other across a table on which the mike was placed. I liked it especially because what I saw was exactly what was going on—one person interviewing another. There was no disembodied voice, I could see the interviewer ask a question, the answer was directed to someone who was *there*, and I saw how that answer was received. In such a format, if the interviewer wanted to show something up close, it would make perfectly good sense to go get the camera ("Wait a minute, let's get a good close look at that") and then later put the camera back where it was. Bad production technique, perhaps, but good ethnography.[10]

How about having a second person along to handle camera? Presumably that would allow you to concentrate on your interviewing, and that presumption could be correct, *so long as you and your helper have the same agenda.* I had a still photographer along with me once. I had seen her work and knew she was good, but quite understandably what she wanted was beautiful and dramatic pictures, and as a result I could never be sure where she was or what she was doing. She was neither pushy nor demanding, but I found that she engaged a surprising amount of my attention along the way. Later, I discovered that the interviewee had a similar reaction, and both of us were relieved when she had to leave early. The moral is that you and your camera handler must plan carefully.

Some Special Problems

The Recording of Music. I have already distinguished between performance and discourse and between natural and artificial contexts, and since the recording of music is always the recording of performance, frequently in an artificial context, I suggest re-reading those paragraphs now. Since you will be going to see someone *because* he or she is a singer or fiddle player, you should go with the best equipment you can lay your hands on. Now is when DAT will really be able to strut its stuff, or, failing that, it is amazing how much difference a better mike or higher grade of cassette will make. If, however, you are limited to whatever equipment you happen to have, the best advice I can offer is not to let that worry you too much, considering how good middle-range or even inexpensive equipment is these days. Often you can go back later with first-rate equipment, and it is always better to have two recordings than one anyhow.

My own experience is a good place to start here. Given my interest in songmakers like Joe Scott, it is true that I interviewed many men who I knew ahead of time were singers, but more often all I knew was that this man was supposed to have known Scott or simply that he had worked in the woods. In the course of the interview I would ask about songs and singing, and if I got anything like a positive response I'd start probing: "When would there be singing?" "What songs would they sing?" "Do you remember any of them?" If it looked as if he did remember some, especially if he mentioned some titles, I'd ask him to sing one for me. Chances are there would be some initial resistance: "My singing days are over." "I don't know that I could get it all together." "I've got this cold," and so on. Then I had to decide whether he was really saying "No" or just needed to be coaxed a bit. Coaxing was and still is part of our musical tradition. (Think of it this way: would *you* sing for a stranger or even for friends at first request, or would you wait to be encouraged a bit? And would you not feel disappointed if people took you at your word and didn't coax you some?)

I can't tell you how to coax someone, but I can offer a couple of gimmicks that I found useful. My first ploy would be, "Look, I wish you'd give it a try. Tell you what: let's record one song, and then you can listen to it back. If you don't like what you hear, we won't do any more." If that succeeded, I can only tell you that I never had a man refuse to go on to more songs because he didn't like what he heard, but if it failed, I had a fallback: "Well, would you just say it over for me?" Then, after he had recited it, I'd try to get him to "sing over a couple of verses so I can get the tune." Occasionally that would be enough to encourage him to sing the next song right through. Finally, if I got a rather clear "no" at one point, I'd move on and bring the request up again later.

The line between the "no" that could mean "yes" and the "no" that really means "no" is not always a clear one, but it is there. Obviously you should not badger someone who clearly cannot or will not sing, but keep in mind many people not only need to be coaxed, they *expect* to be.

Spend some time talking about each song, asking questions like, "Where did you learn it? From whom? Is it about something that really happened? Did you ever know anyone who used to make up songs?" And so on. Naturally I had specific songs I would ask for, and you may very well have too, but it is also interesting to see what songs people come up with on their own. This can result in some interesting insights into taste, repertoire and concepts of categories. On that last point, while I had heard scholars and students talk of Child ballads and broadside ballads, I found that singers spoke of pirate songs, war songs, comical songs, ditties. As a matter of fact, I only heard the word "ballad" used twice in my life, both times to refer to printed copies of songs.

In addition to what I have already said about improved equipment and better cassettes, there are a couple of further comments to be made. Be especially careful not to over-record. Sometimes I have asked a singer to give me a stanza or two so I could establish a good recording level, and it is a good plan, unless in your judgment it will make a singer who is already nervous feel just that much more "on stage," hence more nervous. If you would rather not go to this trouble, for whatever reason, simply turn the gain down (say from "one o'clock" to "twelve o'clock" or even a bit more) just before the interviewee starts to sing. Since people usually sing louder than they talk, chances are that this will give you a workable level. Don't worry if your interviewee sings softly at first, especially an older person who has not sung for a long time. That is a very common pattern.

As a rule, don't adjust the level while the song is going on. Of course, if the singer drives the needle into the red most of the time, cut the gain down right away. But that is an emergency measure. Simply avoid the strong temptation to fiddle with the gain during the song in order to get the perfect level. Wait until the song is over, then make an adjustment in anticipation of the next song. Since dynamics (louds and softs) are an important aspect of musical sound, any change in recording level during a performance will obscure them. For the same reason, by the way, never use automatic level control in recording music (unless you happen to have one of those machines that has nothing else, in which case you are stuck).

Using Photographs and Drawings. Photographs, drawings, diagrams, and maps can add whole new dimensions to your interviews, or they can be an egregious waste of time. The difference is chiefly in how carefully and completely they are coordinated with and identified on the tape. That is, if a photograph is discussed during the interview, it must be clear which photograph it is, where the researcher can find it, and what within the photograph is being described. Actually this is simply one more application of the trialogue concept.

Three kinds of photographs are useful in interviews, and the same basic rules apply to all of them. First, there is the photograph you take yourself—of the interviewee, of the context, or of some object being discussed. It always helps someone listening to the tapes to have some idea of what the interviewee looks like; pictures of the home (both inside and out) and neighborhood may be even more helpful. While some interviewers spend almost as much time taking pictures as they do interviewing, others (myself for one) seldom bother with a camera at all, but there is no question in my mind that portrait and context photographs are valuable.

On the other hand, photographs of objects under discussion are often an absolute requirement. It is hard to imagine, for example, a successful interview about quilting that did not include clear photographs of patterns and techniques. Take your time with such photographs, and work out some system of identifying each one on the tape. If you take your pictures during the interview, you can simply say, "Wait, let me get a picture of that," and then add, "This is my picture number one." You may even pose the picture ("O.K. Show me just how you hold that knife now") or get the interviewee to point to some special feature you are discussing. You may find, though, that the camera gets in the way during the interview, in which case you can take your pictures all at once later on. If you choose this method, I suggest leaving the tape running during the photograph session. Your conversation about each picture and its specific details will thereby serve as a complete and numbered record of your photographs ("Would you hold up that log cabin quilt for me? Picture number four. . . . Fine. Now, how about pointing to that square you had so much trouble with? Picture number five. . . ."). Then follows an extremely important step: after your photographs are processed, you must not only work out a storage system that will make them easily available to the researcher, you must also coordinate the numbers you assign the photographs with those that appear in your catalog. More about that in a moment.

The second kind of photograph is the one you supply in order to elicit comments. Photographs can be great memory-joggers, but they have to be used carefully or they wind up creating horrendous frustrations. What are we to make of this little exchange, for example:

K: Can you tell me what this is in the picture?
P: Why sure, that's a water cart. Now, see, the rope would go up over

there and out this way and then they'd hitch the horses on and they'd go out this way and the barrel'd come up full of water and. . . .

First of all, what picture? Where is the rope that went "over there?" (Where?) Which way was *this* way? The potential for confusion, here, is obvious. And even if *you* manage to understand what all this means, no one else will. So let me offer two simple rules.

Always identify each picture. For example, since each photograph in the Northeast Archives' files is numbered, all we have to do is give that number on the tape ("O.K., here's Archives photo 274. What's that. . . ."). If you use a photograph from a book, cite it clearly ("I've got a copy of Doerflinger's *Shantymen and Shantyboys* here, and there's a picture facing page 233 that I'd like to ask you about . . ."). Then make sure that all the "this here's" and "that fella there's" and "this way's" are clarified. For example, the photograph so frustratingly described in the preceding paragraph is Northeast Archives photo number 29 (see below). If your interviewee (pointing) says the rope went "up over there," you can add, "You mean up over that triangular thing on the top of the box?" If he should identify one of the men ("Well what do you know! There's old Jack Furey. We used to . . ."), you add "The one with his arms folded, right?" I have even found that it helps if I prepare questions about a photograph ahead of time, since in the heat of the interviewee's description, I frequently forget what it was that I wanted to know about the picture in the first place.

The third kind of photograph that is apt to become part of an interview is the one supplied by the interviewee. Say the interview is going along nicely, when suddenly the interviewee says, "I think I've got a picture of that right here" and produces a photograph album. The two rules (Identify and Describe) still hold, but you are going to have some trouble with the first one unless you can borrow the photograph for copying. If the interviewee is willing to let you do this (and that is the way it usually works out), get the work done and the photograph returned promptly. Your archives will probably have a copying service; if not, you may be able to locate a copier elsewhere. Either way, don't let borrowed material sit around too long. If the interviewee is unwilling to let you borrow the photograph, perhaps you can make arrangements to copy it on the spot (at the Northeast Archives, for example, we have a portable copy stand and camera for just this purpose).

Not every photograph is going to be worth copying, of course. You will have to make some judgments here, and sometimes you will not

Plate 1. Water-cart or road sprinkler for icing logging roads. Photograph reproduced by permission of the Northeast Archives of Folklore and Oral History.

be able to tell immediately which photographs are valuable and which are not. I have spent a lot of time looking through piles of old photographs, while the tape was running, because there did not seem to be any alternative. Then I would see one I wanted ("Hey, can I borrow that one to copy it? I'll get it back to you next week. O.K., we'll call this one number one. Now, what's this. . ."). On the other hand, sometimes, since it all seemed so irrelevant to my purposes but so relevant to the interviewee's, and since it looked like we were going to spend some time with the old album, I have shut the tape off (with some explanation such as "Look, I do want to look at these with you, so I'm just going to turn the machine off for a while"). Then take a few notes on photographs you do want and ask for them. Put a temporary identifying number on the back—lightly, and in pencil (felt tip pens can bleed through, and ball point or a pencil used with any force at all will permanently scar the print!). Later on, when you have started the tape again, you can go through the same process as described above ("I'm going to call this photograph number one. Now what did you say was going on here?"). These numbers will then go into your catalog, and when more permanent numbers are assigned to the photographs, you can simply add them in the proper place (photo #3: NA 277). Just remember not to cross out the temporary numbers, because they are still the numbers on the tape.

The same techniques should be used with maps or drawings, which will be taken from similar sources (your diagram, one from an outside source, or one prepared by the interviewee). I should offer one warning on maps though: don't be surprised if the interviewee has no idea how to read a map. I remember one old river-driver who knew every island in the Penobscot from Medway to Old Town, but when I showed him a map of the area, he could not figure it out at all. All his life he had seen those islands from the level of the water; a bird's eye view meant nothing to him. Even if you have prepared maps at hand, it is frequently worth your while to ask the interviewee to draw one (another one of the reasons why you bring plenty of paper and a pencil with you, always). You will be surprised what such maps can tell you about someone's sense of space (what is near and what is far) and direction.

As a general rule, don't introduce photographs or drawings too soon. If possible, hold off on them until the second interview. If there will only be one interview, hold them until the later stages of it. That is to say, don't introduce them before that time. If the interviewee does, it is best to follow that lead and go along. But all too frequently interviewers bring out photographs before they are really ready for them. This is especially true of beginners, who may feel quite ill at ease and are only too glad to have something specific to talk about. Try not to panic into pictures. Take your time. You will do a better job for it, believe me.

While we are on the subject of visual materials, I should tell you what one man, Ernest Kennedy of Argyle, did for me. He wanted to make the operations of the Argyle Boom perfectly clear, and I arrived at his house one day to find that he had built a five-foot-long model of it! During the rest of the fall, as our interviews continued he made models of an endways log raft, a driving dam complete with sluice, a batteau, a yard with a parbuckle, and a whole lumbercamp, all of which we spent parts of several interviews talking about, and all of which he gave to the Northeast Archives! That made the identify and description problem no different from what it would be with a drawing or a photograph, but knowing the mutability of things I am also filing a detailed batch of photographs carefully keyed to the interviews. Ernest's generosity deserves no less.

On-site interviewing. Someone says, "Come on, hop in the car and I'll show you right where that was," or, "I've got one of those out in the barn. Want to see it?" It sounds like a great idea, and it is, providing you keep in mind the same twin problems that exist for any "visual": identification and description. It may be necessary to include a careful map with your transcript, in order to make clear exactly where the interviewee took you, and you may find it helpful to "talk" the route right onto the tape as you move along ("We're heading down 178 toward Charlton. Now we're turning to the left three miles out of Wells, and there's a big white church on the corner. . . .") Then you can retrace your path later, or you can check it on a state highway atlas or a "topo" map. Of course, if you expect to do much of this sort of thing, take some time in advance to learn what features the map is apt to show, then refer to them wherever you can.

Once you are on the site, the problem is the classical one of adequate description, along with some good probing, thus:

A: Now right here's where the old station used to be I was telling you about.
B: [*Into mike*] We're about a hundred feet down the track to the left of where the old road crosses. [*To "A"*] Nothing much left to show it, is there, except for the clearing and all that crushed rock. How big a building was it?

Look hard for things to ask about ("What's that big iron drum over there?" . . . "Where did the road come to then?"). And of course, if you have a camera, use it: have the interviewee point to something, take a photograph, and record an explanation on the tape.

For most on-site interviews, it will probably pay you to come back later and do some more careful mapping. In this regard, I recommend learning how to take an accurate compass bearing. It is simple enough, and it is amazing what you can do with just a compass and a good steel tape (and a ruler, protractor, and pad of graph paper to record your results).

Speaking of maps, I found one special kind of on-site interviewing to be very successful. I once wanted to get an idea of what a particular stretch of road was like seventy years ago, and I asked the interviewee if he would be willing to drive along that road with me and describe it as he remembered it. We started at the town line, where I set my trip odometer at zero, and then we talked our trip onto the tape something like this (my "asides" into the mike are indicated in italics):

> Now right here there was a big farm-house (A: *1.4 miles on left.* How far back?) Oh seven or eight rods. That was the old Hawkins place. Charlie Hawkins was one of my oldest friends. (A:*1.7, crossing a brook.* Did this brook have a name?) No, never did that I knew. It usually dried up in August. Now right here's where Bob Coffin had that store I was telling you about (A:*2.1 on right.* Nothing there now.) No, his son moved it down the road to his place about twenty years ago. You can see there now, that shed next to the barn (A: Oh, yeah. *Big white house, green trim, center gable, barn, shed. 2.6 on right.* What was his name?) Sterling. Sterling Coffin. Got killed in the war. Now over there. . . .

Almost certainly you will want to go over the route again by yourself, once you have made your "map," in order to check distances, add details of your own, and so forth. And before you set out with your interviewee, try recording by yourself in order to find the most workable level. Finally, I can only recommend this technique for back-country work, unless you have a friend do the driving (not a bad plan in any case). Try it on a busy village street and you will either have an accident or get a summons, or both. (Explain that one to the judge!)

Group interviews. Any time you take on more than a single interviewee at once, you have a group interview. The group may be unexpected, as when you go to see a woman, and her husband is not only present but eager to talk too (Good luck to you on this one!). It may arise at the interviewee's suggestion ("My brother Floyd lives just two houses down, so I'll ask him to be here too. What I don't remember, maybe he will"). Or it may be your idea to bring two or three people of like interest together to see if they can "get each other going."

The inspiration for a group interview is usually honest enough. What folklorist has not found himself in a situation where half a dozen people are telling stories either in that time-honored natural context of enlightening the stranger or—and this less frequently—in that even more natural context of having cheerfully forgotten the stranger was there. And you the folklorist sit silently, the hair on the back of your neck rising with your pulse rate, thinking, "Oh, if I only had my tape recorder here *now!*" I remember saying that once while driving round trip from Newcastle to Sackville, New Brunswick, with two fine singers and a bottle of Lamb's Navy Rum. My two friends roared out song after song, telling great stories in between. Yet deep down I knew that if I had the tape recorder there, it would not be the same at all (unless I had "sneaked it," and I have already made my attitude on that kind of shabbiness perfectly clear).

In all cases, the group interview raises special problems which, while not unsolvable, can be exasperating. First of all, there are the technical problems like where to place the mike to pick up both voices, and if there are more than two the problem gets geometrically worse. Transcription is made at least equally more difficult, as you try to identify voices or separate out what two people are saying at once. But problems of this order should not turn you against the technique, for it not only may work, it may work splendidly. The real problem that often spoils group interviews is quite simple: one person dominates, and it is not always the person who really knows the most. This self-appointed spokesman will interrupt, talk over, and even contradict the others to the point where they volunteer less and less, even though you try to draw them out. In other words, you wind up, in effect, with a one-on-one interview anyhow, only with the wrong interviewee. If you are skillful enough to handle this sort of situation, fine; you may even create a more natural context than would be possible in a one-on-one interview. I never have had much luck with it, though, which may in part explain my preference for one-on-one interviews in the first place.

I have sometimes found a group interview useful for a start, a first interview which I can follow up with individual interviews ("Look, the other day when I asked how Breakneck Hill got its name you started to talk when Harry cut you off. What were you going to say?"). Listen closely to the tape of that group interview, and you will find all kinds of leads and clues, but in the end, the burden of the work for tape-recorded interviews will be the one-on-one interview.

More than one interviewer, or "taking a friend." Many interviewers feel the need for a companion, especially when they are going for their first interview with a total stranger. It is hard to recommend against anything that makes ice-breaking a little easier, and therefore I will not advise against it, even though I see the straight one-on-one situation as basic. The presence of a second interviewer is not so much a *bad* idea as it is the cause of special problems you ought to keep in mind both before deciding to invite someone else and, once you have so decided, during the interview itself.

Obviously it will make a difference *whom* you take. Sometimes the person who recommended the interviewee will volunteer to go along, and that may sound innocent enough, but it can happen that the interviewee will spent most of the interview talking to the old friend, not to you. Such an arrangement may be worth your time, though, just for the entrée; you can always go back again. Sometimes, though, the volunteer local "broker" can put you in a bind. I remember one woman up in New Brunswick who offered to take me around and introduce me to some great singers she knew, and the results were nearly disastrous. Not only did she turn out to be just the wrong person (though as an outsider I had no way of knowing that), but since all the real singers in that culture were men, my introduction by a woman was hardly to be taken seriously. It may, of course, be all but impossible to refuse this sort of help, and perhaps the best advice that I can give is that you accept it—it could be great!—but keep an eye to leeward.

The man/woman relationship will be important too. If you are a girl and you take your boyfriend with you to interview a man, if you are a boy and you take a girl with you to interview an old railroad worker, if you are a girl and take a boy to interview a farm wife, or if you are married and take your wife or your husband along, it *will* make a difference. But there is no need to assume that that difference will be negative or restrictive. In fact it is very interesting, in any such situation to notice who captures the interviewee's attention. One girl told me that even though she was "officially" the interviewer and asked all the questions, the man she was interviewing directed every answer to her boyfriend. On the other hand, I remember one time when I took one of my female students with me to interview an old river-driver, and while he directed his answers to me, for the most part, he answered *her* questions in more detail than he did mine. It is impossible to predict what difference the presence of a companion of the opposite sex will make in your interview, but the difference can tell you a lot. Again, don't be afraid of it; just be alert to it.

One special problem (especially, I have found, in husband/wife visits) occurs when the interviewee's spouse is also present: two conversations get going at once, the husband talking to the man, the wife talking to the woman. This situation usually arises out of the couple's desire to be hospitable, but it does not always remain hospitable. I have seen men obviously annoyed when their wives kept "butting in" or "going on," even though they were "going on" to my wife and I have known men who have become very restive and noisy when I showed much interest in what their wives might be saying to my wife. For the purpose of collecting folklore, these "double interviews" can be very fruitful, but on tape they can be chaos. One of the simplest solutions to this kind of crosstalk is to try to split the two pairs; the interviewer's wife, for example, might show interest in something in the kitchen and thereby move her conversation out there.

The age of your companion can make an important difference too, and I will close this section with an example. One young woman wanted to interview an elderly woodsman, and since her uncle had worked in the woods she thought it would be a good plan to take him along. The two men did not know each other, but they soon discovered what a lovely time they could have teasing her by sharing all kinds of silent understandings. As she asked questions, the interviewee would give cryptic answers and then wink at the uncle, whereupon they would both chuckle. This went on for over an hour, while she grew more and more frustrated and angry. When she told me about it, two days later, she was still steaming. "What I really wanted to do," she said, "was decapitate the two of them with a rusty crosscut saw I'd seen in the shed!" If she had, before any jury of her true peers she would have been acquitted.

Obtaining a Release

A release is simply a signed statement by the interviewee that he or she understands the terms under which the interview took place and is willing for the results to be used according to those terms. Most archives require releases and have their own forms which you will be requested to use, but even if you are working independently you should consider getting some form of release. Samples of Northeast Archives releases are printed in the Appendix, and you may wish to model yours on them, but there are as many forms of releases as there are archives.

Many interviewers find it hard to ask for a release, feeling that it is an imposition or even an impertinence. I know I hated to ask at first, but as time went on and neither I nor my students encountered any refusals, I found it bothering me less and less. Now it is routine, though still a part of the routine I wish I could dispense with. But I will not, and you should not. After all, you will mention it in your explanation at the beginning of the interview, and if there are going to be any objections, they should surface at that time. But very seldom will there be any objections at all. Just wait and see.

When you should you get the release signed? I used to suggest getting it at the end of the entire series of interviews, but it too often happened that I would plan to get back for more interviews with someone and for any of a number of reasons never did, which meant that I would have interviews for which there were no releases at all. On the strength, then, of my own experience, I suggest getting a release *at the end of every interview*. Of course, that may mean you will have half a dozen releases from the same person, but that is no problem. An interview for which you have no release *is* a problem—if not for you, at least for your archives.

Most interviewees will accept and sign a reasonable release without hesitation, but for some reason, yours may have reservations or wish to restrict access to or use of the interview. That is, of course, his or her right. Both of you "own" the interview equally, since it was your joint creation, and both of you must be satisfied as to its disposition. There may be good reason why the material in the interview should be restricted, and if, after talking it over with your interviewee, you feel those reservations are reasonable, see what sort of restrictions are suggested. Work it out, but if you feel the demands are excessive, you will have to decide whether to go ahead with the interview. I mentioned above that, since the interview is the joint creation of you and your interviewee, both of you have equal rights in it. Your archives, therefore, will probably ask you to sign a release too (see the Northeast Archives form in the Appendix), and you may have your own restrictions to impose. If you are working on a book, for instance, it would be perfectly reasonable for you to ask that no one else be permitted to publish material from your interviews for five or even ten years, until you have had a chance to do something with it yourself. But don't be a dog in the manger. In the world of scholarship, the more open things can be, the better for us all.

A Final Word on Interviewing

This chapter has been replete, resplendent, and (who knows) maybe even refulgent with suggestions on how to conduct interviews, all of it good advice, and all of it derived from years of experience. But there is one last thing that will be a comfort to remember: just as there is no such thing as the perfect marriage, or the perfect crime, or even the perfect rose, there is no such thing as the perfect interview. You will never listen to a tape of one of your own interviews and not be at least a little dismayed at your blunders ("Why didn't I ask. . . ," "Boy was that ever a dumb question. . . ," "I shoulda followed that up. . . ," etc.). I have never had an interview in which I translated every "over here" or "about this long" the way I know I should, and some of the photo descriptions I have elicited are, sad to say, useless jumbles of "this-heres" and "hims." But in spite of my acknowledged foot of clay, I have been shambling down the road for better than three decades, and in that time I have done some pretty good interviews—some of them, if I may say so, remarkable. My final bit of advice is to get on with it, then. It is all right to be dismayed at your blunderings, so long as you accept them as inevitable and go ahead. It's a good road to travel.

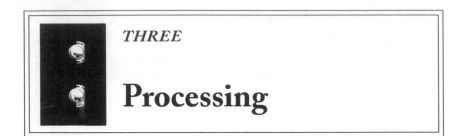

THREE

Processing

The Primary Document

That was the exciting part: going out and interviewing someone. What follows is far from exciting: making the resultant tape a useful and usable primary research document. That takes time and careful, systematic work, but if you skimp on it, you might just as well have stayed home in the first place. There are many different approaches to this processing, and while I will go into most detail on the way we do the work at the Northeast Archives, I will try to give enough information about other approaches to make an intelligent choice among them possible. But since the approach you choose will depend heavily on what you decide is the primary document, we should spend a little time defining that term.

A primary document is one behind which there is nothing. A letter or a diary, for example, would be a primary document, while versions of them reproduced in a book—no matter how carefully done—would be secondary documents. By analogy, then, it would appear that the tape recording should be looked on as the primary document and any transcription of it considered secondary. While that is essentially how I conceive of them, there are two important qualifications, one theoretical and one practical, that I would like to make.

In theory, the tape recording is still a secondary document, because *the interview itself* is primary, the tape being no more than the best available record of that interview. But since there is no way yet available of returning to the interview itself, the point is moot. On the other hand, if what you do is to transcribe the interview and then send the transcription to the interviewee for correction or amplification, and if the interviewee does in fact make alterations—deleting passages, adding fuller explanations, correcting sentence structure, and the like—then the resultant manuscript becomes the primary document, the tape and transcript merely rough drafts. In this situation, if you want to find out what the interviewee "said" about something, you would not go to the tape but to the corrected transcript.

As a general rule, oral history archives have emphasized the importance of the final transcript, and while the tapes are usually retained in some fashion, they are very seldom referred to. Folklore archives have generally taken the opposite approach; not only is the tape the working document, there are often no complete transcriptions, and even the catalogs may offer only a bare outline of the tape's content. At the Northeast Archives of Folklore and Oral History, we have tried to take a middle ground. While we consider the tape as the primary document, we also want some kind of secondary record of what is on that tape, but, whether that record is a brief log of the tape's contents or a complete transcription, its purpose is to facilitate finding material on the tape itself. In other words, we want researchers to listen to the tape either to check whatever transcriptions we have available or to make their own. So long as the tape is available, the transcript should never be treated as an end in itself.

No question about it, though, a transcript makes the best record of what is on the tape, calling attention to items that are far too brief or peripheral to appear on any log or summary. But transcription involves a rather large investment of time or money—time if you do the work yourself, money if you hire someone else to do it. You can count on it taking ten to twenty hours to transcribe an hour of interview, depending on how technical the subject is, how clearly the interviewee speaks, and (here it is again!) how well you placed the mike. Some people enjoy transcribing; others (I am one) find it tedious. Either way, it is an extremely important part of the job, and you should get it taken care of as promptly as possible.

Making a Transcript

Like it or not, the ideal person to transcribe an interview is you, the interviewer. You were there, you've had direct experience with the interviewee's speech patterns, and presumably you know what he or she was talking about. If, for instance, there are significant gestures or unexplained measures of distance—and in spite of your best efforts there *will* be some—you are the only one who will be able to make sense of them. Not only that, but the transcription process, by forcing you to listen carefully to what went on, will help you plan for future interviews. And finally, I know of no better way than self-transcription to teach what good interviewing is and is not, what succeeds and what does not. Students invariably report that transcribing their first interview is a kind of catharsis, sometimes embarrassing but always chastening and edifying.

What equipment will you need? In a pinch, you can use your recorder, but since transcribing requires a great deal of stopping, backing up and restarting it is apt to be rather tough on the switches. I recommend that you use a transcribing machine with a foot pedal control. There are several varieties on the market. Most of them have an automatic backspacer, which means that when you stop the tape it backs up a few inches (how far is usually adjustable), allowing you easily to relisten to a troubling passage. Headphones (usually the machine comes with a set) are not absolutely necessary, but almost always they will allow you to hear the tape more clearly. A final monition: in deference to Murphy's Law, it's best not to work with the original cassette. Make a copy.

If you are blessed with the skill of shorthand, that is certainly the most efficient way to make your first draft, but failing that I will unhesitatingly recommend that you use a word processor. I am a latecomer to the faith, but the ease with which these contraptions allow you to make additions and corrections (and you will have to make many!) is nothing short of remarkable. I can all but guarantee that using one will cut your transcribing time by a quarter or even a third over what straight typing or longhand would take. Almost any good word-processing program will do the job, so long as it has both italic and regular format and a key for brackets ([]), but, since those are pretty standard, that is not much of a problem. On the other hand, your printout raises two problems. First problem: legibility. Since you will want to be able to photocopy (especially if your material is going into an archives), make sure the print is dark enough. Many of the dot-matrix printouts I have seen are too light. Second problem: durability. Your transcript may get a lot of handling. Therefore, use a good quality paper, something that will stand up (I'd recommend twenty-pound bond), preferably "non-acidic" or "pH neutral" for longer shelf life. And never use "erasable" papers; they have a nasty tendency to smear.

When you set up to transcribe, keep a pad of paper next to your keyboard for jotting down questions you will want to ask, and *jot a question down the minute it comes into your head!* Believe me, that statement is important enough for italics and an exclamation point. Do not "make a mental note" to jot it down "as soon as you finish this sentence," and by no means count on a review of the completed transcript to suggest questions. Either way, you will forget. Keep that pad right at hand, and take the time to write your questions out clearly ("Jam-breaking with dynamite. Here he says they placed the charge 'a ways back' from the face. Earlier he said 'at the face.' Which?" Rather than "dynamite: where placed?") You'll be surprised how cryptic the latter question will have become by the time you go back for a follow-up interview. If there are names, spellings or technical terms you're not sure of, make a note of them to remind you either to look them up or to ask the interviewee about. Believe me, that "pad right at hand" is one of your most important research tools.

As I mentioned earlier, as a good general estimate it takes about fifteen hours to transcribe an hour of interview. Some people can do it in less (the best time I ever heard of was six hours), some take longer, but the point is it involves many hours of intense concentration, and, if you are going to do your own transcribing, it is important to determine what your "transcribing threshold" is and arrange your time to accommodate it. For instance, I find I can go about an hour—two hours tops—before I have to break to something else: walk the dog, have some coffee, write a letter, anything at all. If I try to push beyond that limit I get sloppy and impatient. In fact I turn the whole thing around and use stints of transcription as "breaks" between other tasks. On the other hand, I know people who can go at it all day straight out. Factoring your limits into the amount of work you have to do and whatever deadlines you may have to meet will go a long way toward helping you keep sane.

In preparing to transcribe, one of the first things you should decide is the level of accuracy at which you intend to work. This decision will be largely dictated by the purpose the material will serve in your research. A dialectician will be concerned with pronunciation; a historian probably will not be. A psychologist doing pausal analysis will be interested in the length of every pause and the exact number and location of every "uh" and "er"; a folklorist might not require this kind of detail at all. The archives or program for which you are working may have requirements of its own, of course, which you will have to accept. What follows are the instructions we at the Northeast Archives give to people doing their own transcriptions for deposit with us. They strike a kind of middle level of accuracy that we have found adequate for most purposes, since the assumption can be made that the tape is easily available to anyone requiring more detail.

Even under ideal circumstances, a transcript is simply the best representation you can make of what is on the tape, but since it *is* a representation, it is unavoidably an interpretation. No two people will transcribe the same tape in exactly the same way, even if they are following the same set of guidelines, nor will the same person transcribe it in the same way on two different occasions (try it and see). We must accept this sort of variation as inherent in the whole process, but accepting it as a limitation in no way invalidates the process itself. Rather, the process is strengthened, because we will use it more intelligently, knowing as we do what can reasonably be expected of it.

At the top of the first page of your transcription, set down essentially the same information you put in your opening announcement. Something like the following will do nicely: "Interview with Horace Davidson, Mattawamkeag, Maine, April 13, 1988. Interviewer is Thurlow Blankenship and this is his tape number 78.5." Following that, if you plan to use initials to identify the different speakers in the body of the interview, you should identify them here, thus: "B = Blankenship; D = Davidson." I also recommend that you include three short paragraphs, the first describing briefly the content of the interview, the second its context, and the third the level of linguistic detail represented by the transcript. For example:

> Davidson, 87, had been a steam locomotive engineer on the Canadian National Railway for many years. In this interview he tells of his youth, his brief experience as a seaman, and his first railroad job.
>
> His daughter, Mrs. John LaRue, in and out, was watching television in the adjoining room. Truck traffic on U.S. 2 gets rather loud at times. Used Sony TC-5000 with RE-15 mike on table about 2' away.
>
> Davidson makes many false starts, which I have eliminated along with his frequent interjection of "you know." Noise of fluorescent light overhead is constant.

These sample paragraphs, by the way, are very brief. You can go into much more detail on any one or all three. It is impossible to overdocument an interview. At Northeast Archives we have developed a "cover sheet" which takes care of this information very well (see Appendix).

After setting this "front matter" off by something like a a row of asterisks, begin the transcription proper. If you are typing, I would still recommend double-spacing to make it easier to pen in corrections later, but with word-processing it is not necessary. Use dialogue form, thus:

> B: Did you ever have any close shaves?
>
> J: Close shaves? You mean like did I almost ever get myself killed? Well, only once that I can recall, but that was enough [*laughs*].

B: What happened that time?

J: You want to hear about that, do you? All right. . . .

Set all material not actually on the tape in italics and enclose it in brackets. You may want to explain an extraneous sound [*loud bang at this point caused by cow exploding outside the window*] or describe a gesture [*demonstrating: clasps hands over head*]. Or you may wish to describe some important off-tape action [*When he said this his wife shook her head "No" from the other room*]. One of the most important functions of such "stage directions" is to explain why certain passages are unintelligible. It may be that something went wrong with the tape recorder or that the interviewee's granddaughter came into the room and turned the television set on, drowning out the interview. In all such cases, your note should be full enough to really explain what happened:

B: What did you use for that?
J: Well, you'd use a crimper. I think I've got one right here in this [*at this point, Mrs. Jones started looking through a lot of utensils in a drawer in the table we were sitting at, and the noise makes it impossible to hear what she is saying for about ten seconds*] used to be right in there. Well, anyway, etc. . . .

Even under the most ideal circumstances, though, there will inevitably be words, phrases, and even longer passages that you simply will not be able to understand, in spite of the fact that you conducted the interview yourself. The Northeast Archives rule-of-thumb here is that if you cannot get it after three good tries, move on. It is futile to keep going over and over the same passage. Your best bet is to call someone else in; a fresh pair of ears can make all the difference (my wife Bobby has frequently saved the day this way). If even that doesn't work, though, leave some indication that material has been left out and get it behind you for now. If you're typing, leave a blank at least as long as—and preferably longer than—the troublesome passage, so that you or someone else could fill it in later. With word processing, all that is needed is some way of indicating something has been omitted; I recommend [-?-] or perhaps just [*unintelligible phrase*]. You will catch many of these puzzlers by going through the tape (as you should) a second time.

Inevitably comes the question, "Must everything be transcribed—every word, every sound? The answer is yes, but a qualified yes: *transcribe everything in accordance with the level of accuracy at which you or your archives intend to work.* At the Northeast Archives, we used to insist on the transcription of all "uh's," all backing-and-filling, all false starts, and all tag questions ("you see?" or "know what I mean?"). We no longer require such detail, partly because we found it practically impossible to transcribe consistently (some "uh's" and "y'knows" were always left out) and partly because of our conviction that the tape is the primary document and anyone requiring that level of accuracy would be a fool to trust someone else's transcriptions. For example, someone following our old instructions would have had to transcribe a passage as follows:

> K: Did you ever work on, well, on other rivers besides the Penobscot?
> J: Did I what uh, did I uh well, let me think uh yeah now sure yeah sure
> I uh drove the uh uh the Kennebec River one no it was one spring yes.

We would now suggest that passage be transcribed this way:

> K: Did you ever work on other rivers besides the Penobscot?
> J: Well, let me think. Yeah, I drove the Kennebec River one spring.

The passage may be a bit extreme to begin with, but not all that extreme: you will get many like it. If you do have an interviewee who responds in this halting manner, say something about it in your headnotes.

Another omission we have decided to permit is interviewer interjections. We used to insist on their inclusion, enclosing them in parentheses in order not to break up the narrative flow, thus:

> B: We were coming down that hill just beyond Lily Bay there (I: uh-huh), and the road was just a little slick. It had rained the night before, see (I: yeah), and it was still a little cold that early in the morning, know what I mean? (I: oh, sure) Well, etc.

Once again, we feel that someone interested in such supportive devices should be working directly from the tape. However, if you decide you want to include them, our old system works very well.

Sometimes a pause can be as significant as anything that is said, maybe significant enough to be in the transcription. There is no hard and fast rule here; you will have to exercise some judgment as to whether a pause is meaningful or just part of the interviewee's speech pattern. It may, for example, be significant that the interviewee hesitates for some time before he answers a question, if you have determined that he *normally* does not do that. Indicate such important pauses by giving their approximate length:

> J: We were stuck out there on that little center jam and the water was rising and we was in one hell of a fix I tell you. Then a man by the name of—oh, what was his name? [*pause: 10 sec.*] Well, it don't matter none now, but he etc.

How about dialect? There are strong differences of opinion as to whether one should try to represent pronunciation by altering spellings, but we at the Northeast Archives strongly recommend that you stay away from any representation of dialect in transcripts. Don't write "wa'p" when you know the interviewee would probably spell it "warp" for example, or "jest" for "just," and don't leave off final "g's" (write "going," not "goin'"). Transcribed dialect always contains within it an element of condescension, and you will never have to apologize for or "explain" the use of standard spelling. And for heaven's sake, keep away from eye dialect ("wuz" for "was"). Dialect is important, but a transcription should not be made to bear the burden of it. Once again, if researchers are interested in this level of detail, they should be working with the tapes, and your transcription can show them just where on the tapes to look.

Given these exceptions—tags, interjections, false starts, dialect—the basic rule is still valid: Get everything down that is on the tape. Don't record what you think the interviewee *meant* to say; put down exactly what he did say, without "correcting" grammar, usage, or sentence structure. Nine times out of ten it will be perfectly clear how you should handle a passage, but you will inevitably have to make some decisions. Take the following passage, for example:

> J: I don't know, I don't know that I ever had a a tougher job a tougher job handed me. But the uh the uh two of us, him and me, him and me together, we—on that unjeczily job, all winter we was man and man about.

I would be inclined to transcribe the passage as follows:

> J: I don't know that I ever had a tougher job handed me. But the two of us, him and me together on that unjeezily job, all winter we was man and man about.

This preserves grammar, word order, and usage (a word like "unjeezily" is a word, but you will have to decide how such words should be spelled). I would consider the following version as taking too many liberties.

> J: I don't know that I was ever given a tougher job, but he and I worked man and man about on it all winter.

How do you handle two people talking at once? One of the best ways I know is to separate the two speeches to the best of your ability; then connect them with a hand-written brace in the margin, thus:

> J: Did the fire ever get this close to town?
> { Mr.: Oh goodness, yes, it burned Herman Jones'—
> { Mrs.: No, I don't think that fire ever did. He's thinking about the 1948 fire. Now that one, etc.

The brace (you will have to explain this in your headnote) would indicate that both Mr. and Mrs. were talking at once, while the dashes would indicate that he broke off while she continued. If the confusion is too great for this convenient device to bear, you may simply have to explain in a stage direction: [*Mr. and Mrs. Smith were both talking together here, and it is very hard to tell what is going on, but the gist is that he felt it had while she was sure it had not*].

As I have said already, no two people will transcribe a passage in exactly the same way. That variation from transcriber to transcriber will be nowhere more evident than in the matter of punctuation; one person will use a period where another person will use a comma. Punctuation marks (Victor Borge to the contrary notwithstanding) are conventions of print, and in making a transcription you will adapt them to represent the conventions of spoken language (pauses, alterations of pitch and loudness, and the like), which means once again you will have to make judgments. Work them out as best you can. Usually you can "feel" sentences clearly enough, and that can tell you where to put your periods and question marks. And since a lot of people begin sentences with conjunctions, don't feel compelled to comma a speech into one vast run-on sentence in obedience to a school-teacher rule that says you must not begin a sentence with a conjunction (a silly rule, almost as silly as the one that says a preposition is something you shouldn't end a sentence with). If the interviewee drops his or her voice and pauses in a way that tells you *that* sentence is over, put a period. Two hyphens (—) can be used to show where an interviewee breaks off or was interrupted. Work out the rest of the text with commas and semicolons. Use exclamation points sparingly, and the same can be said of using capital letters for emphasis. There is only one absolute prohibition: don't use a series of spaced periods to indicate anything in a transcription. These are standard ellipsis marks, indicating that something has been left out, three (. . .) indicating less than a sentence, four (. . . .) indicating more than a sentence. They will have their place when a researcher quotes a passage from a tape or transcription in a published work, but their inclusion in a transcript could be confusing. Any omissions in a transcript (and as a rule there should be none) should be fully explained, both as to content and extent, in brackets and underlined.

In order that the transcript be as useful and convenient as possible for finding material on the tape, you should cite digital counter calibrations every so often. Put them in the body of the text and circle them in black, thus:

R: We'd go across the river on the logs, thousands and thousands, all full of spruce gum. And we'd pick chunks of spruce gum and we'd come down and sell it to Burnham Drug Company. (0435) Somedays we'd go fishing too, etc.

On a word processor, it is easier to set the numbers in boldface. Be sure to indicate what machine (make, model, and even the specific machine, if possible) you used for the calibrations. Following your transcript, and using your calibrations, researchers will find it relatively easy to locate the desired passage on the tape. And that is what we want to encourage them to do!

How do you transcribe songs or poems? Begin with an indication such as [*sings:*] or [*recites:*]. Then listen to the whole song or poem and try to "fetch out" the lengths of lines and the stanza structure. It is not as hard or as arcane a task as it might seem. Most people, including almost all of those who claim they are "tone deaf" (which they really aren't), can handle it by listening for pauses—short at the ends of lines, longer at the ends of stanzas—and the places where the tune seems to "break some" (at the end of a line), "come to an end," or "start over" (at the end of a stanza). Try it a few times. Then get a friend to try it, or compare the stanza form you fetched out with what someone else may have used in publishing that song in a collection. The following is a good example of how your transcript should look:

> I: I was wondering if you ever heard a song called "The West Branch" or some call it "John Roberts."
> K: Yes, sure, I've heard it, and I think I even know it all. Let's see, how did that begin now [*pause: 10 sec.*] Yeah, O.K. now [*sings:*]
>
>> John Roberts as I understand
>> He was a brave and fine young man
>> He hired out with Mr. Brown
>> To help him bring his lumber down.
>
>> Up the West Branch he then did go
>> It proved his [*pause: 5 sec.*] proved his sad overthrow
>> He ventured out to break a jam
>> And fell beneath the rolling dam.

Ultimately, the tune should be transcribed too, but that is a whole new subject involving special skills, techniques, and training. Unless you are such a specialist, just keep a good record in the transcript of where the tunes are that will need transcription.

I have already alluded several times to the fact that you should always make a final check of your transcript by listening to the tape once more and following it through on the transcript. This second check is very important. Not only is it possible that you will find things you neglected to transcribe the first time (it doesn't happen often, but it happens), and you will also find that many previously unintelligible passages will suddenly become perfectly clear.

So far I have assumed that you will be doing your own transcribing. How will it change things if you hire someone to do the job for you? No question about it, it will save you many hours of hard work, but in no way will it relieve you of responsibility for the quality of the final product. You can't simply land the cassette on someone and say, "Here, do it!" First of all, you will have to make sure that the transcriber knows exactly what it is you want in regard to completeness and detail. Do you want everything on the tape, or should false starts, repetitions, tag questions, interviewer interjections, and the like be left out? How about "stage directions?" Single or double spacing? (Single-spacing will be fine if the transcriber's and your processing programs are compatible, allowing you to make corrections right on the disk. Otherwise I'd recommend double-spacing the first draft, since for sure you are going to have to make corrections. The final draft can easily be reformatted to single-space.) And so on. In addition, you should prepare a duplicate cassette—never work from the original!—and along with the cassette should go a log of personal and place names, technical terms, and the like (all correctly spelled) that the transcriber might have trouble with. If there are places where the volume suddenly increases, where there are sudden loud noises, or where there are technical glitches, you should give ample warning.

Second, once the transcript has been completed, you will have to check it carefully against the cassette for completeness and accuracy, and you can count on this process taking two or three hours for each hour of interview. A few pages back I said that while transcribing you should keep a pad of paper handy to write down questions for the next interview. Since you obviously couldn't carry out this review then, do it now. It is an extremely important step in the interview process. Don't slight it.

Should completed transcripts be shown to interviewees or sent to them for corrections, deletions, and (who knows?) amplifications? That is one of the standard procedures for many oral history programs, and while we at Northeast Archives always allow for this privilege if requested, it is not part of our normal processing. The interviewee's release reminds users that they are "reading a transcript of my spoken, not my written word, and that the tape, not the transcript, is the primary document." We consider the transcript completed when the interviewer has corrected it for the last time. But under any circumstances, if interviewees want copies of cassettes or transcripts—for whatever reason or for no reason at all—that settles it: they get what they ask for. We send a photocopy. If it is returned to us with changes, as a rule we file both the original and the corrections. If, by the way, your sixth sense says the interviewee might make this request, you can mention the possibility in your opening explanation.

Final Disposition and Future Use

At the beginning of the first chapter, the research method described in this book was said to consist of two separate but interrelated activities: first, the holding of extended taped interviews, and second, the processing of those interviews so that their contents will be easily available to both yourself and others. We have now covered the fieldwork proper and as much of the processing as would usually be carried out by the interviewer. The next step should be to get the material—cassette, transcript, documentation, etc.—into an archives, preferably one that understands and has facilities for handling tapes and their transcripts.

That brings me to an important bit of advice: When it comes to doing fieldwork in folklore and oral history, don't make a fetish out of your independence. I know how easy that is to say and how hard it is to avoid. As fieldworkers, most of us are pursuing some special interest, and we tend to get rather possessive of the territory our quest opens up to us, guarding it zealously against possible poachers, talking about "our" informants, and the like. I know that the idea of depositing my material in something other than an egg crate in my locked closet just didn't set right at first, but I allowed myself to be persuaded, and there have been no problems.

There are three good reasons for getting your material into an archives. The first has to do with preservation: Not only will an archives' physical facilities be better than yours, the very fact that you will certainly keep working copies means that your material will be in two places rather than one. Thus, if there is a fire or if you should accidentally erase a tape, another copy is always available. The second reason has to do with access: Subject to whatever controls you wish to impose, scholars and other interested parties will find it far easier to use your material—either in their own work or to check the accuracy of yours—if it is in a public repository rather than solely in your personal possession. The third reason has to do with reference and is really a corollary to the matter of access: If you are working through an archives, you will be able to reference your oral materials through their system of citation, making it far easier for others to follow up on or check your work. In this regard, it is a good plan to begin working with an archives as early in your project as possible. As an archivist, I often hear people say they will deposit their material in Northeast Archives "as soon as they're through with it," and I do my best to persuade them not to wait that long, both for safety and for simpler citation. You have everything to gain by archival deposit and nothing to lose.

There are many repositories where you might reasonably place your material, ranging from the local library or historical society right up to and including the Library of Congress, and where you should put it will depend heavily on who you think should have access to it. A project whose main object is to increase a community's awareness of its own past obviously should make the materials it generates easily available locally, say in the town library, while a more focused, more "scholarly" project might be appropriately placed in a more specialized archives, say at the state university. There may be good reason, too, for making duplicate deposits; if, for example, you are concerned about the security of material you have left in the local library, a backup deposit in a state archives might be a prudent idea. Whatever you decide, you should be satisfied that a repository is set up to handle oral materials. A college library that has neither special listening nor storage facilities might make a poor choice. The American Folklife Center (Library of Congress, Washington, D.C. 20540) is always glad to tell you what archives are available in your area, and Allen Smith's *Directory of Oral History Collections* (see the Bibliography) is an excellent resource, but it never hurts to do a little quality checking on your own.[11]

On the Publication of Oral Materials

The tape recording as a research document is still a comparatively new concept, and while forerunners of the technique can be found even as far back as the late nineteenth century, it has really been with us no more than forty years.[12] Within those years, though, it has burgeoned, being used by many people for many different purposes, and has been subject to almost as many codes of conscience as there have been users and uses. As a result, when we pick up a book or article and read something taken from a tape recording, we are seldom given any indication of its accuracy—that is, how close it is to the interviewee's actual words—and we are almost as seldom given any way to check that accuracy for ourselves. It is my contention that readers must always be given both just as carefully as they would be given them for a quotation from a written or printed source.

But the problem is not quite as simple as it is for printed sources, where we have had both a long tradition of standard citation procedures and a strong tradition that insists on quotations accurate to the comma and letter. For the oral source, citation is not really much of a problem, since we can easily adapt the footnote and reference systems already used for printed sources. The real problem is accuracy, because, as we have already seen in our discussion of transcription, the question arises as to how accurate we intend or need to be. At the very least, authors owe readers a clear and complete statement of their methods.

It should be assumed that you the author are responsible for the transcriptions, either having made them or having checked existing transcriptions against the tape. If you are working from a transcript which you have not so checked, say so, and to the best of your ability describe what that transcript represents. If the transcript contains more than is on the tape—for instance, if it has been edited by the interviewee and includes his or her corrections and additions—you should make that very clear. In addition to all this, you should say what level of accuracy you have aimed at, what emendations you have made, and how such emendations are shown. Finally, you should indicate where the original tapes and transcripts are on deposit and how and under what circumstances they may be consulted (this should include a description of your system of citation). I offer the following as a model:

> All quotations preceded by an asterisk are taken verbatim from a tape recording: false starts, "uh's," and the like are the only material that has been eliminated without an indication of the omission by standard ellipsis marks. Within these verbatim passages, brackets indicate that the speaker's words were not absolutely clear, but this is my best guess as to what he was saying. In some places I have added words of my own to clarify a passage or to include a "stage direction." All such additions are both italicized and bracketed. Quotations not marked with an asterisk are taken as accurately as possible from field notes, but I cannot guarantee word-for-word accuracy.
>
> The tapes and their accompanying transcripts are on file in the Northeast Archives of Folklore and Oral History, South Stevens Hall, University of Maine, Orono, Maine. Accession numbers (e.g. NA 423) are given in every case, and reference is given to page numbers in the catalog or transcript whenever possible (e.g. NA 423.157). Duplicate copies are on file in the Archive of Folk Culture, American Folklife Center, Library of Congress, Washington, D.C.

The techniques given in the above model are ones that I have found very workable, and to the best of my ability I impose them on all work, student and professional, coming out of the Northeast Archives. I have, by the way, found the technique of distinguishing taped from untaped quotations by marking the former with an asterisk very useful, since I have never yet written either a book or an article for which all the relevant data miraculously got recorded. But the exact techniques are less important than the recognition of the basic concept: that readers have a right to know exactly what they are dealing with, and the author has an obligation to give them that information.

Appendix

A Compendium of Forms Used
by the Northeast Archives of
Folklore and Oral History

UNIVERSITY OF MAINE *at Orono*

Department of Anthropology
Northeast Archives of
Folklore and Oral History

Stevens Hall, South
Orono, Maine 04473
207/581-7466

July 31,1973

Mr. John O'Connor
RFD # 2
Old Town, Maine

Dear Mr. O'Connor:

For many years the Argyle, Nebraska, and Pea Cove Booms
played an important part in the social and economic life of
this part of Maine, but they are swiftly becoming no more
than a memory, and it won't be long before they are not even
that. For things that were once so important, it is amazing
how little information is available in libraries or anywhere
else on just how boom work was done and what it was like to
work on one. The Northeast Archives is therefore making a
special effort to remedy this situation by talking to as
many people as can be found who used to work on the booms.

A couple of days ago I was talking to Tom Burns up in
Howland, who said that you had worked on Argyle Boom for
many years and that if anyone could tell how the work went
you could. Would you be willing to let me come around and
talk to you about it? I am sure that you could add a great
deal to our knowledge of boom operations, and I hope you'll
agree to see me. I will be in touch with you in a couple of
days. Meantime, thanks for any consideration you can give
my request.

Sincerely yours,

Thurlow Blankenship
Research Assistant

*Plate 2. This is the basic letter we used for making our first contact with possible
interviewees for the Argyle Boom project. It is a reasonable model for
any such letter.*

A(10/25/76)

NORTHEAST ARCHIVES OF FOLKLORE AND ORAL HISTORY
South Stevens Hall
University of Maine
Orono, Maine 04473

        In consideration of the work the Northeast Archives
of Folklore and Oral History is doing to collect and preserve material of value for the study of ways of life past
and present in the New England-Maritimes area, I would
like to deposit with them for their use the items represented
by the accession number given below.

        This tape or tapes and the accompanying transcript are
the result of one or more recorded, voluntary interviews
with me. Any reader should bear in mind that he is reading
a transcript of my spoken, not my written word and that the
tape, not the transcript, is the primary document.

        It is understood that the Northeast Archives of Folk-
lore and Oral History will, at the discretion of the
Director, allow qualified scholars to listen to the tapes
and read the transcript and use them in connection with their
research or for other educational purposes of a university.
It is further understood no copies of the tapes or transcript
will be made and nothing may be used from them in any
published form without the written permission of the
Director.

                        Signed: *Martin Callaghen*

                        Date: *July 11, 1978*

Understood and Agreed to:
Interviewer: *Thurlow Blankendie*   Date: *July 11, 1978*
Director: _____   Date: _____

Accession number: _____

*Plate 3. This is our standard release form, the one we use about 95 percent of the
time. It gives the Archives the most discretion, which makes it the most desirable
from our point of view.*

7/29/74)

NORTHEAST ARCHIVES OF FOLKLORE AND ORAL HISTORY
South Stevens Hall
University of Maine
Orono, Maine   04473

In consideration of the work the Northeast Archives of
Folklore and Oral History is doing to collect and preserve
material of value for the study of ways of life past and
present in the New England-Maritimes area, I would like to
deposit with them for their use the items represented by the
accession number given below.

This tape or tapes and the accompanying transcripts are
the result of one or more recorded, voluntary interviews with
me. Any reader should bear in mind that he is reading a
transcript of my spoken, not written word and that the tape,
not the transcript, is the primary document.

It is understood that the Northeast Archives of Folklore
and Oral History will, at the discretion of the Director,
allow qualified scholars to listen to the tapes and read the
transcript and use them in connection with their research or
for other educational purposes of the university. It is
further understood that no copies of the tapes or transcript
will be made and nothing may be used from them in any published
form without my written permission, until _*July 11, 1983*_
after which time the Director's written permission will be
required.

                          Signed: _Martin Callaghan_
                          Date: _July 11, 1978_

Understood and Agreed to:

Interviewer:

Thurlow Blankenship   Date: _July 11, 1978_

Director:

_____   Date: _____

Accession Number_____

Plate 4. Release form B gives the Archives permission to let people listen to the tapes
and examine the catalogs or transcripts, but it leaves control over publication and
the making of copies with the interviewee.

C(7/20/73)

NORTHEAST ARCHIVES OF FOLKLORE AND ORAL HISTORY
South Stevens Hall
University of Maine
Orono, Maine 04473

In consideration of the work the Northeast Archives of Folklore and Oral History is doing to collect and preserve material of value for the study of ways of life past and present in the New England-Maritimes area, I would like to deposit with them for their use the items represented by the accession number given below.

This tape or tapes and the accompanying transcripts are the result of one or more recorded voluntary interviews with me. Any reader of the transcript should bear in mind that he is reading a transcript of my spoken, not my written, word, and that the tape, not the transcript is the primary document.

I desire to place the following restrictions on this material. That no use of any kind whatsoever is to be made of this material until ___*July 11, 1983*___.
After that time it is understood that the Northeast Archives of Folklore and Oral History will, at the discretion of the Director, allow qualified scholars to listen to the tapes and read the transcripts in connection with their research or for other educational purposes of a university. It is further understood that after that time, no copies of any kind will be made of the tape or transcript nor will anything be used from them in any published form without the written permission of the Director.

Singed: *Martin Callaghan*

Date: *July 11, 1978*

Understood and agreed to:

Interviewer: *Thurlow Blankenship*   Date: *July 11, 1978*

Director: _____   Date: _____

Accession number: _____

Plate 5. Release form C is used when the interviewee wishes to "close" the accession for some specific length of time. Until the given date, no one may either listen to the tapes or examine the catalogs or transcripts thereof.

D(8/7/75)

NORTHEAST ARCHIVES OF FOLKLORE AND ORAL HISTORY
South Stevens Hall
University of Maine
Orono, Maine 04473

       This tape or tapes and the accompanying transcripts
are the result of one or more voluntary interviews held
by me with (name)___Martin Callaghan_____
(address)_____Argyle, Maine_____.
Any reader of the transcript should bear in mind that he
is reading a transcript of our spoken, not our written,
words, and that the tape, not the transcript, is the primary document.

       Although he did not sign a formal release, it is my
understanding that the interviewee has no objections to
this material being used according to the terms of Form
__A__, a copy of which is attached to this form, with the
following exceptions:

                              Interviewer: _Thurlow Blankenship_
                              Date: _July 11, 1978_____

Understood and agreed to:

Director: _____   Date: _____

Accession number:_____

*Plate 6. Release form D is an entirely "self-serving" document which we use
when the interviewee expresses willingness to have the material used but refuses
to sign anything. Naturally, we prefer not to use this form, but occasionally
it has been necessary.*

NORTHEAST ARCHIVES OF FOLKLORE AND ORAL HISTORY
South Stevens Hall
University of Maine
Orono, Maine 04473

Interviewer Agreement

    I,   Thurlow Blankenship   , in view of the historical
      (Interviewer: type or print)
and scholarly value of the information contained in the inter-

view(s) with   Martin Callaghan
          (Interviewee(s): type or print)

and designated as accession number   1243   , knowingly and volun-
tarily permit the Northeast Archives of Folklore and Oral History
the full use of this information, the tapes and transcripts and
all other material in this accession, and hereby grant and assign
to the Northeast Archives of Folklore and Oral History all rights
of every kind pertaining to this information, whether or not such
rights are now known, recognized, or contemplated, except for such
restrictions as are specified below.

July 11, 1978
   (Date)

                    Thurlow Blankenship
                    (Interviewer's signature)

Restrictions:

Understood and agreed to:

                        (Director)

                        (Date)

*Plate 7. All interviewers sign one of these releases, usually after
having completed a series of interviews.*

NORTHEAST ARCHIVES OF FOLKLORE AND ORAL HISTORY
TRANSCRIPTION COVER SHEET

Interviewer's tape no.: 78.3   **NAFOH Accession No.:** 1243   (T1738)

Interviewer: Thurlow Blankenship **Address:** 172 No. Fourth St., Old Town, ME

Interviewee: Martin Callaghan   **Address:** Argyle, ME (RFD #2, Old Town, Me.)

Place of interview: MC's home   **Date of interview:** 11 July 1978

Equipment used (include both recorder and mike): UHER 4000 Report L with

ElectroVoice RE-15 mike.

Tape: Brand: 3M AV-176   **Size reel:** 5"   **Thickness:** 1½   **Speed:** 1 7/8

Cassette: Brand: C30 60 90   **Type: I II IV**

Dolby: ~~In~~ Out. B C   Mono ~~Stereo~~

Amount of tape or cassette used: (Side 1): all   (Side 2): 1/3

Interview context (Where? Others present? Problems? Etc.): Held in kitchen.
Mike in small stand on stove, about 2' from MC. No-one else present, except that
MC's son came in with some groceries about halfway through side 1 (tape turned
off for about 5" during his stay.

Brief description of contents: A continuation of a series of life-history
interviews. This time MC tells of his one winter lumbering on the Allagash,
1912-13.

Transcriber: Thurlow Blankenship   **Date of transcription:** 20 July 1978

Level of accuracy represented by the transcript: Since MC speaks slowly and
distinctly, the transcript is quite accurate. But I have not included his
frequent use of "uh" and "you know."
B= Blankenship
C= Callaghan

Plate 8. One of these forms is completed by the interviewer for each interview.

Blankenship 78.3   1.

[Opening announcement]

B: When would you say you left home? (C: Well--) Or wasn't there any one time or

C: No, the only time I--I was always back and forth to home. I never stayed away for over
a year. I went away, I went up on the Allagash. Let me see now. *[pause 10 sec.]* **0018**
Yeah, I went up to the Allagash. I went up in Aroostook County potato picking time in the
fall, another guy and I, and we picked potatoes up there.

B: When would that have been? Have you any idea?

C: When it was? (B: Yeah) Well, I think that was 1912 or 13, somewhere along there. I
went up there to pick potatoes. Didn't like it. Stopped. And it come a rainy spell, an awful
rainy spell, and we was losing a lot of time picking potatoes, so I said "The hell with it. We
might just as well go somewheres into the woods." So we settled up with him, old Fred
Dube we was working for in Winterville.

B: He was working with you? (C:Eh?) Fred Dube, you say? He was working with you?

C: No, for him. He was a farmer, and we was picking potatoes for him (B: Oh, I see.) in a
place called Winterville, this side of St. Francis before you come to Eagle Lake. **0040**
Anyway, we quit there and went up to Fort Kent, the other guy and I.

B: Who was the fellow you went with?

C: Ed Blackett. We went up to Fort Kent, and we hung around there a few days, and we
ran into a fellow up there that was going up the Allagash lumbering. He was looking for
men. He was just a young man, and we used to hang around a bar there was there. In Fort
Kent there was a foot bridge which went from Fort Kent right across the river to Claire,
New Brunswick, just a narrow foot bridge. And right at the end of that foot bridge was a
barroom. (B: On the Claire side?) On the Claire side. There was a great big room there, had
a bar there on one side of it where [--?--] used to hang around town, you know, so we
used to hang around there, and this guy come in there. **0057** He was from St. Francis. He
was hiring men, wanted men to go up on the Allagash. We talked with him and he said,
"You fellows want to go up for me? What do you do in the woods?" Said, "I can do most
anything I have to do. I can cook, and I'm a teamster," I says, "and I can do most anything
else, but I'd rather cook or drive a team." So he says, "Well, I got a young fellow wants to
go up and cook, a young man, and he's supposed to be quite a good cook. He worked at it
quite a lot. He wants to go up and try it," he says, "but you go up, and if he can't handle it,
why you can take over. But if he can handle it, you can drive team."So we went up, and
the young fellow done all right. **0070** So I drove team. Worked there all winter. *[At this
point Callaghan's son dropped in for a visit, and the recorder was turned off for ten
minutes or so]*
      B: O.K. Here we go again. Now you were saying you just met this guy in that
barroom and hired right there. Is that right?

      C: Yup. His name was Baptist Jalbert, and there was four or five brothers of them,
and they was all woodsmen. The other brothers took charge for the Cunliffe Lumber
Company. That's who I went up there for, the Cunliffe Lumber Company in Fort Kent. So

Plate 9. A sample transcript, part 1.

I took a pair of horses right there in Fort Kent, green team they'd just brought in there. I took them and drove them up the Allagash. We hooked them to a wagon and went up to the mouth of the Allagash up where it come into the St. John's River. There was a place there, kind of a lodging house, a big farm. Pelkeys their name was. Put up people going back and forth, woodsmen. **0090** Anyway, we got there that night and we stopped there all night. They said that we was going to take the boat in the morning. Well, I was green to that country; didn't know how they done business, and I see the mouth of the river there was all just low water, rocks. And I says I don't know what kind of a place they're going to go with a boat here--I said that to myself [*chuckles*].

In the morning we got up and went down, and that's the way they towed it, in scows, with horses. They were flat-bottomed scows as long as from here out to the road there. (B: That long? Maybe forty, fifty feet?) Yeah , forty, fifty feet. They'd take twenty-five tons of stuff on it, provisions and stuff. [*phone rings. Not his ring*]

B: It wouldn't draw much water.

C: Wouldn't draw much water. She'd go anywheres in there on the river. Sometimes she'd drag on a gravel bar. They'd have a big pair of horses out front on a line and boy they'd walk her right along. Walk her just as hard as they could go at it. And they had a channel, all the rocks rolled out. They had a channel all the length of the river there. That's the way they done their toting. They had a half a dozen of them boats on the river, different people, to tote stuff for the town or something like that.

Anyway, next morning I went down to see what they had, then. This scow was a long scow. Had a railing about three feet high on each side. On top of the side there would be a railing on top about eight inches wide.

B: It went right around the whole thing, eh?

C: Yeah, right around on both sides. The front end was like a scow. it picked up like this, you know, it slided iup like this [*swooping his right hand upward in a curve*] two or three feet above water where it come up. On the hind end of that they had a little cabin that looked almost like this room. About as big as this room [*about 15' by 15'*]. And I cooked in there. And I lived in there with the scow crew. I was the cook and everything as long as I was in there. There was only about four men to a scow crew. **0140**

They had a long tow line on the head end of this scow. The horses was about [-?-] out ahead of this scow on this line.(B: Maybe fifty feet?) Fifty feet. They had little short whiffletrees there across the back just down to the side for them. Then we'd hook right on to the harness, so they would stay right up there, you know.

B: Whoa, wait a minute. I don't quite see how that worked. Could you draw that for me?

C: Well, let me have that paper. Now [*drawing. See drawing number* 月] that rope went like this, see, right across the front and hooked on to them little whiffletrees this way, here, and another one here. (B: O.K. Good) A man rode them on horseback, on a saddle, one man. Pair of horses. He'd ride one. That rope hooked on the front end of the scow. Then back about ten feet from the front they had a mast like, pole up there about ten feet high. It had a little truck like, on the top of that. It had a rope went up through that truck--just a common half-inch rope--and tied it about halfway out on that line they was towing.

This channel is kind of crooked in places. **0175** Some places they'd go across the river, and where they made a swing there might be a rock or an old deadhead log or something sticking up. That [*tow*] rope would catch it. That rope lay right on the water,

Plate 10. A sample transcript, part 2.

NORTHEAST ARCHIVES OF FOLKLORE AND ORAL HISTORY
SOUTH STEVENS HALL
UNIVERSITY OF MAINE
ORONO, MAINE 04473

REQUEST FOR USE OF ARCHIVES

Name: _J. ROBERT PIGOTT_   Date: _JULY 23, 1978_

Address: _54 COLLEGE AVENUE, CLINTON, NEW YORK_

Describe as completely as you can the sort of material or the
specific items you are looking for. If you are interested in a
particular town or other geographical area, be sure you mention
that too.

_I AM LOOKING FOR INFORMATION ON HOW LOGGING
ROADS WERE MAINTAINED IN GOOD SHAPE THROUGHOUT THE
WINTER. I AM ESPECIALLY INTERESTED IN THE YEARS
BEFORE WORLD WAR I._

What use do you plan to make of this material? Are you writing a
book, article, dissertation? Are you a teacher who wants material
for lecture or classroom demonstration? Please be as specific as
possible.

_THIS MATERIAL WILL BE USED FOR A CHAPTER IN A
BOOK I AM WRITING ON CHARLES MORRISSEY, ONE TIME
MAYOR OF GLENS FALLS, N.Y., AND A WELL-KNOWN PROHIBITIONIST
IN UPSTATE NEW YORK. IN HIS EARLY YEARS HE HAD
WORKED IN THE MAINE WOODS AS WHAT HE CALLED A
"ROAD MONKEY," WHICH HE DESCRIBED AS SOMEONE WHO
KEPT THE LOGGING ROADS OPEN._

I understand that all material is the property of Northeast
Archives of Folklore and Oral History and cannot be reproduced or
published in any form or way without the written permission of
the Director. I also agree to bear all costs of xeroxing, photographs, and tape publication in connection with my request.

Singed: _J. Robert Pigott_   Date: _JULY 23, 1978_
****

Disposition:

*Plate 11. Anyone wishing to use the Archives completes and signs
one of these forms first.*

Notes

1. For an interesting adaptation of stereo equipment to recording what is going on in something like dance, where the music is recorded on one channel while on the other channel the field worker describes what people are doing, see the two articles by Ivan Polunin listed in the Bibliography.

2. This advice on "starting at home" should be balanced against what is said about "stranger value," in the section on *The Initial Contact*.

3. See my *Larry Gorman: The Man Who Made the Songs* (Bloomington: Indiana University Press, 1964; rpt. New York: Arno Press, 1977; rpt. Fredericton, New Brunswick: Goose Lane Editions, 1993); *Lawrence Doyle: The Farmer-Poet of Prince Edward Island* (Maine Studies, no. 92 Orono: University of Maine Press, 1971); *Joe Scott: The Woodsman-Songmaker* (Champaign: University of Illinois Press, 1978).

4. Edward D. Ives, *Argyle Boom* (Orono, Maine: *Northeast Folklore* 17, 1976).

5. For a good discussion of this performance/discourse continuum, see William Hugh Jansen, "Classifying Performance in the Study of Verbal Folklore," in *Studies in Folklore in Honor of Stith Thompson*, ed. W. E. Richmond (Bloomington: Indiana University Press, 1957), 110–18.

6. Kenneth S. Goldstein, *A Guide for Field Workers in Folklore* (Hatboro, Pa.: Folklore Associates, 1964), 80–87.

7. Neil Rosenberg has suggested that, in recording performances in their natural context, one should place the microphone where it can pick up the full ambience of sound—audience coming and going, people talking and ordering drinks, pinball and cigarette machines operating, etc. See his article, "Studying Country Music and Contemporary Folk Music Traditions in the Maritimes: Theory, Techniques, and the Archivist," *Phonographic Bulletin* 14 (May 1976): 18–21. This has been reprinted in his booklet, "Country Music in the Maritimes: Two Studies," Memorial University of Newfoundland Department of Folklore, Reprint Series, no. 2 (1976). His comment is worth quoting in full: "Whenever possible,"

he said, "I recorded events: Dances, fiddle contests, jam sessions, house parties, radio sessions, and rehearsals. In most of these situations I used an omnidirectional microphone and set the recorder at slow speed, so as to record the total audio event" (rpt., 15).

8. For the story of my discoveries of these three songmakers, see my *Larry Gorman*, especially 2–7; *Lawrence Doyle,* especially xv–xviii; and *Joe Scott,* especially xxi–xxvii. See also my *George Magoon and the Down East Game War* (Champaign: University of Illinois Press, 1988; rpt. 1993), 32–45.

9. Raymond Gorden, *Interviewing: Strategy, Techniques and Tactics* (rev. ed., Homewood, Ill.: Dorsey Press, 1975), 422–44.

10. Significant sections of this interview may be seen in Jeff Todd Titon's "Albert 'Hap' Collins of South Blue Hill, Maine" a videotape issued by the Maine Folklife Center, South Stevens Hall, University of Maine, Orono, Me. 04469.

11. In Canada, check with the Canadian Centre for Folk Culture Studies at the National Museum of Civilization, Hull, Québec.

12. The earliest published use of recorded materials is probably J. Walter Fewkes's "A Contribution to Passamaquoddy Folk-Lore," *Journal of American Folk-Lore* 3 (1890): 257–80.

A Brief Bibliography

This list is not exhaustive. It simply includes a few items that I have found helpful. I have also tried to include items on oral history that most folklorists might not know about and a few general works on folklore for the benefit of oral historians. Many of these works have good bibliographies of their own, to which the reader can refer.

Agee, James, and Walker Evans. *Let Us Now Praise Famous Men.* New York: Ballantine Books, 1966 (first published 1939). Read it. That's enough said.

Allen, Barbara, and Lynwood Montell. *From Memory to History.* Nashville, Tenn.: American Association for State and Local History, 1981. Covers the use of oral history in historical research, in many ways taking up where the present book leaves off. Covers the relationships between oral and written sources, testing for validity, and producing a manuscript from oral sources.

Alten, Stanley R. *Audio in Media.* 4th ed. Belmont, Calif.: Wadsworth, 1994. A technical book that any interested non-technician can understand. The chapters on sound, acoustics, and equipment are especially useful. A marvelous book.

Baum, Willa K. *Oral History for the Local Historical Society.* 3d ed. Nashville, Tenn.: American Association for State and Local History, 1987. A very good introductory guide. Says a great deal in 62 pages. Bibliography.

———. *Transcribing and Editing Oral History.* Nashville, Tenn.: American Association for State and Local History, 1977. Although written from the point of view of standard elitist oral history programs, this book is not narrowly doctrinaire. Contains a wealth of good advice. Includes a brief recording of an interview and that same interview transcribed. Has a good descriptive bibliography.

Bishop, John Melville and Naomi Hawes Bishop. *Making Home Video.* Wideview Books, 1980. The subtitle, "How to Get the Most from Your Video Cassette Recording Equipment," describes this book well. Although written before the advent of the camcorder, it covers the basics of equipment and technique, and it is full of suggestions for making the best use of video. There is a later version, *Home Video Production*. New York: McGraw Hill, 1986. Unfortunately, both are out of print.

Brunvand, Jan Harold. *The Study of American Folklore: An Introduction*. 3d ed. New York: W. W. Norton, 1986. A good one-volume introductory folklore text, with individual chapters on the various genres, each of which is followed by an extremely useful and descriptive set of bibliographic notes. This and Toelken's are the books I always recommend to non-folklorists as openers.

Colman, Gould P. "Oral History—An Appeal for More Systematic Procedures." *American Archivist* 28 (1965): 79–83.

Dorson, Richard M. *American Folklore and the Historian*. Chicago: University of Chicago Press, 1971. Contains a series of essays by this leading American folklorist on the interrelationships of folklore and history, especially in such areas as traditional, folk, and oral history.

———, ed. *Folklore and Folklife: An Introduction*. Chicago: University of Chicago Press, 1972. See entries below for List, MacDonald, and Roberts.

———, ed. *Handbook of American Folklore*. Bloomington: Indiana University Press, 1983. Over threescore articles by nearly that many folklorists on topics, interpretation, methods, and presentation of research.

Dunaway, David K. and Willa K. Baum, eds. *Oral History: An Interdisciplinary Anthology*. Nashville, Tenn.: American Association for State and Local History, 1984. A huge and useful gathering of articles by scholars from various fields. Covers all aspects of oral history.

Folklife and Fieldwork: A Layman's Introduction to Field Techniques. Revised Edition. Washington: Publications of the American Folklife Center, no. 3, Library of Congress, 1990. A brief (35 pages) guide, telling what to collect, who to interview, and how to do it.

Fletcher, William. *Recording Your Family History*. New York: Dodd, Mead, 1986. Over 300 pages of questions that an interviewer might ask, very neatly categorized—and with a good index. Covers just about all phases of life and family relationships.

Frisch, Michael. *A Shared Authority*. Albany: State University of New York Press, 1990. Critical reflections on the craft and significance of both oral and public history, including some challenging material on what a transcript should be and what happens when oral materials are transformed into public documents.

Georges, Robert A., and Michael O. Jones. *People Studying People*. Berkeley: University of California Press, 1980. "Our basic premise is that an understanding of fieldwork is dependent upon an appreciation for the fundamental human nature of the pursuit," say the authors. Required reading for anyone planning fieldwork.

Goldstein, Kenneth S. *A Guide for Field Workers in Folklore*. Hatboro, Pa.: Folklore Associates, 1964 (also published as American Folklore Society Memoir 52).

While this book seems to be written for the person planning a year's expedition to a foreign country, it is still a useful reference work for those of us who are not. Chapters on problem statement, pre-field preparation, establishing rapport, collecting methods, etc. Bibliography.

Gorden, Raymond L. *Interviewing: Strategy, Techniques, and Tactics.* Rev. ed. Homewood, Ill.: Dorsey Press, 1975. Very complete and readable. Covers much more than just tape-recorded interviews. Good on what makes an interview go well, what gets in the way, probes (especially good!), leading questions. Bibliography.

Grele, Ronald J. *Envelopes of Sound: The Art of Oral History.* 2d ed. New Brunswick, N.J.: Transaction, 1985. Articles by various hands—plus an extended panel discussion—on various aspects of oral history.

Ives, Edward D. *An Oral Historian's Work.* Bucksport, Maine: Northeast Historic Film, 1987. A forty-minute videocassette that covers advance preparations, interviewing, transcribing, and archival deposit by following the author through the entire process.

Jackson, Bruce. *Fieldwork.* Champaign: University of Illinois Press, 1987. A very complete and readable guide, covering all aspects of fieldwork. Good on equipment: microphones, cameras, video, movies. A fine concluding chapter on ethics.

Jolly, Brad. *Videotaping Local History.* Nashville, Tenn.: American Association for State and Local History, 1982. Although written before the advent of the camcorder, this is still a good brief introduction. Some of the advice on video and oral history differs markedly from mine.

Journal of American Folklore. 1888– . The official quarterly publication of the American Folklore Society and one of the leading folklore journals in the world. For subscription and other information write the American Folklore Society, 1703 New Hampshire Ave., N.W., Washington, D.C. 20009.

List, George. "Fieldwork: Recording Traditional Music." In Dorson, *Folklore and Folklife,* 445-54. Selection of equipment, some tips on mike placement. Emphasizes the importance of good documentation. Bibliography.

MacDonald, Donald A. "Fieldwork: Collecting Oral Literature." In Dorson, *Folklore and Folklife,* 407-30. Based largely on MacDonald's fieldwork in Scotland. Emphasizes advance preparations, the recording of contexts, the use of tape recorders, tips for the beginner, directive and non-directive interviews, payment, etc. Very clear and useful. Bibliography.

Moss, William W. *Oral History Program Manual.* New York: Praeger, 1974. Based on the author's own experience in the John F. Kennedy Library's oral history program, this book is essential reading for anyone involved in large programs.

Neuenschwander, John A. *Oral History and the Law.* Denton, Tex.: Oral History Association, O.H.A. Pamphlet Series No. 1, 1985. Gives clear and concise information on legal questions involving oral history.

Notes and Queries on Anthropology. 6th ed. Revised and rewritten by a Committee of the Royal Anthropological Institution of Great Britain and Ireland. London: Routledge and Kegan Paul, 1951 (rpt. 1971). An extended guide to careful field observation and careful description. Intended especially for work with non-literate groups, but its usefulness is not limited to that. Covers all aspects of culture.

Oral History. 1969– . The official and very lively semiannual publication of the Oral History Society, and a good way for Americans to find out what is going on in British oral history. For further information, write the Secretary, Robert Perks, National Sound Archive, 21 Exhibition Road, London SW7 2AS.

Oral History Review. 1973– . The annual publication of the Oral History Association, containing both regular articles on all aspects of oral history and selections from papers delivered at annual meetings. The proceedings of all earlier meetings are also available from OHA. For further information, write the Oral History Association, P.O. Box 3968, Albuquerque, N.M. 87190.

O'Sullivan, Sean (O Suilleabhain, Sean). *A Handbook of Irish Folklore.* Dublin, 1942. Rpt. Hatboro, Pa.: Folklore Associates, 1963. An exhaustive (699 pages) questionnaire covering almost every conceivable aspect of Irish folklore and folklife, and almost all of it is very easily adaptable to our own scene. A good place to turn if you want help in working up questions or in figuring out what to talk about in an interview.

Perks, Robert. *Oral History: An Annotated Bibliography.* London: British Library, 1990. Although intended to be "comprehensive for the United Kingdom and selective for the rest of the world," this book is still very useful for finding American material. It has excellent annotations and a fine index.

Polunin, Ivan. "Stereophonic Magnetic Tape Recorders and the Collection of Ethnographic Field Data." *Current Anthropology* 6 (April 1965): 227–30. A method for recording the "event" on one track while making simultaneous observations on the other. Very clear text and diagrams.

———. "Visual and Sound Recording Apparatus in Ethnographic Fieldwork." *Current Anthropology* 11 (February 1970): 3–22. A commentary with a reply by eight other scholars and a final rejoinder by the author. While the emphasis is on film and videotape techniques, there is enough here on tape recording to make it well worth checking. Bibliography.

Preston, Dennis R. "'Ritin' Fowklower Daun 'Rong: Folklorists' Failures in Phonology." *Journal of American Folklore* 95 (1992): 304–26. Contains some challenging observations on transcription. See also response by Elizabeth Fine (96: 323–30) and Preston's rejoinder (96: 330–39).

Roberts, Warren E. "Fieldwork: Recording Material Culture." In Dorson, *Folklore and Folklife,* 431–44. Contains excellent advice on how to document material objects such as buildings, tools, and the processes involved in various crafts. Bibliography.

Rosenberg, Neil V., ed. *Folklore and Oral History.* St. John's, Newfoundland: Memorial University of Newfoundland Folklore and Language Publication Series, Bibliographical and Special Series No. 3, 1978. Papers from the Second Annual Meeting of the Canadian Oral History Association, October 3–5, 1975. Twelve essays by scholars from various disciplines. The emphasis is on the Newfoundland scene, but the application is universal.

Schorzman, Terri A., ed. *A Practical Introduction to Videohistory.* Melbourne, Fla.: Krieger, 1993. Explores the use of video in historical research, including an overview of technical and archival issues.

Smith, Allen. *Directory of Oral History Collections.* New York: Oryx Press, 1988. A very complete listing of the larger United States collections. Arranged by state, with a good cross-index by subject.

Spradley, James P. and David W. McCurdy. *The Cultural Experience: Ethnography in Complex Society.* Prospect Heights, Ill.: Waveland Press, 1988. "This book is based on the premise that the perspective of cultural anthropology is learned through ethnographic field work," say the authors, who then go on to give very readable and helpful advice on finding a "culture," discovering good interviewees and interviewing them, etc. Included are twelve student papers on everything from a car theft ring to firemen. A fine book. Bibliography.

Stielow, Frederick J. *The Management of Oral History Sound Archives.* Glenview, Ill.: Greenwood Press, 1986. Even if you are not planning to set up on your own, this little book can help you understand the problems archivists face.

Tedlock, Dennis. *The Spoken Word and the Work of Interpretation.* Philadelphia: University of Pennsylvania Press, 1983. While based on the author's work with Zuni and Quiche oral performance, the principles he lays down can be applied to the transcription of oral history. A challenging book and a recommended read.

Thompson, Paul. *The Voice of the Past.* 2d ed. New York: Oxford University Press, 1988. The best general book on oral history yet written. Chapters on all aspects of the craft. Required reading.

Titon, Jeff Todd. "The Life Story." *Journal of American Folklore.* 93 (July–September 1990): 276–92. Sets up some worthwhile distinctions between such terms as life history, oral history, oral autobiography, and, of course, life story.

Toelken, Barre. *The Dynamics of Folklore.* Boston: Houghton Mifflin, 1979. A very readable general introduction to folklore with several chapters directly relevant to fieldwork. Good critical bibliographical essays at the end of each chapter.

Vansina, Jan. *Oral Tradition as History.* A revision and expansion of the author's classic *Oral Tradition* (1965). Based on his long acquaintance with African traditions, he develops and discusses standards for evaluating the historicity of oral testimony.

Wasserman, Ellen S., ed. *Oral History Index: An International Directory of Oral History Interviews.* Westport, CT: Meckler, 1990. Interviews listed by interviewee. No subject index, but includes a list of oral history centers worldwide.

The following books are included as examples of four different ways tape-recorded interviews can be used in published works on folklore and folklife.

Degh, Linda. *People in the Tobacco Belt: Four Lives*. Ottawa: National Museum of Man, Mercury Series, Canadian Centre for Folk Culture Studies, Paper No. 13, 1975. The tape-recorded life histories of four Hungarian immigrants to Canada, with descriptive, interpretive, and analytical commentaries included for each one.

Ives, Edward D. *Argyle Boom*. Orono, Maine: *Northeast Folklore*, vol. 17, 1976. An important aspect of the lumber industry—the sorting and rafting of logs at the end of the drives—that ceased operation about 1930, described in detail by eighteen men who did the work. A very direct application of the methods and principles of documentation put forward by this manual.

Montell, William Lynwood. *The Saga of Coe Ridge: A Study in Oral History*. Knoxville: University of Tennessee Press, 1970. A good example of a local history in which the documentation is almost entirely oral folk testimony. The Preface is a good summary of the debate over the validity of such testimony.

Thornton, Ralph. *Me and Fannie: The Oral Autobiography of Ralph Thornton of Topsfield, Maine*. Orono, Maine: *Northeast Folklore*, vol. 14, 1973. A life history, selected and edited from many hours of tape recorded interview, as reorganized and edited both by the editor and the author himself.

Index